ALSO BY DEAN GOULD

THE GREATEST SALES BOOK EVER WRITTEN
2ND EDITION, 2018

RISE TO THE TOP

HOW TO BECOME A GREAT LEADER, MANAGER, AND MENTOR

DEAN GOULD AND DAVID GOLDIN

ISBN-13: 9780976355311
LCCN: 2018940082

Cover and interior designed by Ellie Searl, Publishista®

Dingo Publishing
Rockville, MD

ACKNOWLEDGMENTS 9

PREFACE 15

INTRODUCTION 19

  1 MANAGEMENT ISN'T FOR EVERYONE 24

  2 GETTING STARTED 29

  3 HIRE WINNERS TO BUILD A WINNING TEAM 31

  4 WINNERS COME IN MANY SHAPES AND SIZES 35

  5 HIRING EXPERIENCE: IS IT ALWAYS NECESSARY? 39

  6 THE STEPS TO TAKE TO HIRE WINNERS 43

  7 TIME KILLS DEALS 51

  8 HOW TO INTERVIEW 53

  9 WHAT TO LOOK FOR IN A GREAT SALES REP 57

10 HOW TO TEAR APART A RESUME 68

11 DON'T MISS OUT DUE TO TUNNEL VISION 74

12 SUMMARY FOR HIRING GREAT PEOPLE 76

13 BE A STUDENT OF THE GAME 80

14 EVALUATE THE TALENT YOU HAVE INHERITED 83

15 THE DREADED FIELD VISIT LETTER (FVL) 88

16 THE PURPOSE OF THE FIELD VISIT AND THE LETTER 90

17   HOW TO PREPARE FOR THE FIELD VISIT.........................94

18   DOS AND DON'TS FOR THE FIELD VISIT 100

19   THINGS TO DISCUSS DURING THE FIELD VISIT 102

20   POST CALL AND FIELD VISIT DISCUSSIONS...............104

21   FORMAT OF A FIELD VISIT LETTER 106

22   RECOGNIZING PERFORMANCE ISSUES 109

23   GO WITH YOUR GUT AS WELL AS THE FACTS..............112

24   BE A GOOD LISTENER...116

25   TECHNICAL OR CLINICAL PEOPLE IN SALES: IS IT GOOD? 119

26   MANAGE EACH PERSON INDIVIDUALLY......................122

27   HOW TO SAVE A TOP REP FROM LEAVING THE COMPANY 124

28   LEAD BY EXAMPLE 136

29   COMMUNICATE WITH YOUR PEOPLE............................139

30   SET SPECIFIC WRITTEN GOALS FOR THE TEAM...........141

31   UNDERSTAND AND HELP ACHIEVE YOUR SALESPEOPLE'S
      GOALS (LONG TERM AND SHORT TERM) 143

32   KEEP YOUR MANAGER WELL-INFORMED ON ISSUES.................145

33   INSPIRE AND MOTIVATE YOUR TEAM AND EACH INDIVIDUAL...147

34   CREATE TEAMWORK 150

35 IMPOWER YOUR PEOPLE TO BE SOLUTIONS-ORIENTED.............. 153

36 GET YOUR PEOPLE INVOLVED IN SALES MEETINGS................... 155

37 HOW TO HELP YOUR NEW SALESPEOPLE 157

38 LET YOUR COLTS RUN, BUT KEEP A REIN ON THEM.................. 161

39 BE STRONG AND BE TOUGH WHEN YOU HAVE TO.................... 163

40 BE A LEADER, NOT JUST A MANAGER 168

41 STAND FIRM TO WHAT YOU BELIEVE.. 172

42 YOU'VE GOT TO BE FAIR 175

43 TROUBLEMAKERS AND NEGATIVE PEOPLE................................ 178

44 KNOW WHEN TO HOLD 'EM; KNOW WHEN TO FOLD 'EM 182

45 THE POWER OF POSITIVE THINKING 184

46 HOW TO DEAL WITH AVERAGE REPS.. 187

47 PUT YOUR REPS FIRST; GIVE THEM THE GLORY 190

48 KEEP AN OPEN MIND TO WHAT OTHERS ARE SAYING............... 194

49 OLD-TIMERS 196

50 GET OUT AND WORK WITH EVERYONE 199

51 BE TRUTHFUL WITH YOUR PEOPLE... 200

52 GIVE CLEAR DIRECTIONS... 201

CONCLUSION 205

ACKNOWLEDGMENTS

Dean:

FIRST, THANKS TO MY WONDERFUL wife, Alissa, for supporting me in everything I do and for being my best friend. What an incredible life and family we have built together. Without her, I'm nowhere. I couldn't have achieved so much without the help, love, and support of my wife. Thanks to my great family, my in-laws, and to my incredible friends who support me through thick and thin.

Over twenty years ago, I met David Goldin, and he literally changed my life forever. I thank him a lot because without him believing in me and giving me a shot in medical sales, who knows what I'd be doing today. I believe that much of what I have achieved today is because Dave was put in my pathway.

In my second edition of *The Greatest Sales Book Ever Written*, I wrote an entire chapter on being grateful and thankful for all the people who have helped you along the way. Well, I certainly owe Dave for the career he gave me. I was out of work—strike one. I had way too many jobs in a short time—strike two. And I had the "wrong" type of sales experience—strike three.

Most medical managers hiring into entry-level positions want people who have sold copiers or who have detailed some sort of product—banging on doors. My sales experience was in real estate and banking. Dave saw past all that and was able to look inside my heart to see a fire in me that would not be stopped. No recruiter would work with me due to the strikes against me. I networked my way, via another Johnson & Johnson Manager, Richard Moorhead, to whom I'm indebted for passing me along to Dave.

Dave was one of the greatest sales managers within Johnson & Johnson, but outside J&J, where I believe he spent half his management career, he racked up countless awards for his leadership as well. There are very few sales managers, or mangers for that matter, who can stack up against William D. Goldin, and I was fortunate enough to be mentored by him throughout my career. So, it only seemed natural that after writing my best-selling sales book, I would have the honor to ask Dave to help me pen a book on becoming a great mentor, leader, and coach. Much of what I know I learned from Dave: a leader who has won Sales Manager of the Year awards seven times in his career. Amazing.

Dave told me his favorite movie of all time is *It's a Wonderful Life* with Jimmy Stewart. Dave's life is a "Wonderful Life." He has directly impacted so many people like me, that the ripple effect caused by this man has positively impacted the lives of thousands of others.

My dad, Gerald Gould, was one of the greatest leaders I've known and someone I learned from throughout my life. The president of several land development companies, he had hundreds of people under his direction who loved and respected him. He achieved tremendous success through his leadership style and business acumen, and he has been an incredible inspiration to me. He was the kind of guy who, no matter what curve ball life threw him, always believed he was going to hit it out of the park; and he did. When life gets tough, I often think of the odds my dad overcame to become such a success.

Of course, my mom, Lois Gould, gave me compassion and understanding for people, and everyone knew she ran the Gould family. What an amazing woman. I've come to realize that most kids eventually become their parents, and I was fortunate to get so much good from my mom and dad.

My father-in-law, Bob Fagan, owned and ran a very successful electronics company, and he and my mother-in-law, Caryn, have been great sources of advice, input, and support. No matter what life has thrown us, they have been there for my wife and me, and I'm so grateful to have them in our lives.

I worked for another successful sales manager, Rick Puleo, who achieved greatness as a manager. He won Sales Manager of the Year and led his teams to success, year after year. I learned a tremendous amount about sales and sales management from Rick. Even though we became friends, he never let me slack and probably raised the bar higher for me than others because we were friends. He knew how to manage in such a way that I never wanted to let him down. Rick taught me to be solutions-oriented rather than just leaning on others.

Debbie Goldstein was my first region director when I became a manager. She gave me my first opportunity to become a manager and provided me with the foundation to begin my management career. She taught me about patience and helped me avoid the frustration many managers experience early on. Often, we feel we are working with some representatives who seem to do everything wrong or "different" from the way we believed they need to be done. Debbie taught me that successful reps come in many different packages.

Charlie Lechner taught me about attention to the details, about follow-up and follow-through as a manager. He showed me that if I had an empty territory I shouldn't be afraid to roll up my sleeves, get out there, and directly sell again. He showed me that being a leader isn't about barking orders and giving direction, but about leading by example.

Jeff Oveland, another region director for whom I worked, is a man who takes a stand for what he believes and what is right. We need fewer "yes" men and women in this world. We need more people who are willing to state, in a positive way, what is wrong, and people who will suggest solutions to make changes for the betterment of companies. Too many companies get bogged down in politics, and nothing seems to get better.

Ralph Larson, former CEO of Johnson & Johnson once said, and I paraphrase, "Change is inevitable, and those companies or individuals who are unwilling to change will become dinosaurs." So many people and companies talk about "openness" and being able to "leave your rank at the door in meetings." Yet, when it comes down to it, very few leaders are willing to hear the truth. As a director of sales, Jeff was always willing to hear the truth and tell the truth.

Manny Asser taught me the power of asking salespeople good, probing questions, to not take everything at face value. Everything is not always as it appears in this world, and Manny was the best at uncovering what was really happening in a situation. Manny was also not one to mince words, which is a quality I like and respect. He would not waste time addressing poor performance and never left a situation incomplete for the next person. Often managers will allow a floundering rep to hang on, leaving the problem for the next manager. Not Manny. He always did the right thing and let people know where they stood.

Chris Schneider, formerly at CarboMedics, was a great all-around leader. He had a great ability to read situations and read individuals and, thus, was a great guy to go into battle with. He would stand up for what is right and wouldn't back down to anyone.

Scott Bell, my last director of sales for whom I worked at CarboMedics, was a great listener and decision-maker. He was supportive and knowledgeable, which every manager needs in order to be an effective leader. He too knew more about our products and the industry than most, but he was also open to hearing new ideas.

Bob Coradini, who has been president of several J&J companies, is another natural-born leader who commands respect from his troops. He's the kind of guy for whom you want to do well and someone you don't want to let down. Talk about positive attitude; there is no one I know who has a better outlook and belief that he will succeed at everything he does. In fact, he seems to succeed at everything he does.

Ryan Hatfield gave me an opportunity to come back to J&J after being gone for six years, which literally changed my life in many ways. First, when my son was born, I ventured into a business I didn't enjoy. Ryan's offer to return came just in the nick of time. In eight years, between Cordis and Acclarent, I was able to triple my pension for when I retire. I came back two weeks before our competitors launched their big products, so it was quite a war; but Ryan put his trust in me and we got the job done. He was a great support and went to bat to help us.

Matt Salkeld gave me an opportunity to work for Acclarent, which was the most interesting and most enjoyable job in my career. He allowed me to run my team as I saw fit, and thus I was able to achieve tremendous success for him and for the company. In collaboration with his leadership team, he helped develop some of the most innovative selling programs, training, and strategies in the industry. It was an amazing period in my career, and I have Matt to thank.

Neal Balius is a great leader—very bright with incredible ideas. He knows how to hire strong leaders, and while he demands a lot, he also knows that life is short, and you've got to enjoy what you are doing. He understands the art and the science of leadership, I learned a lot from him, and I really enjoyed working for him. Neal is a guy you can count on and one who never played politics. He always does what is best for his people and the company, and hence you want to go into battle for him.

My most recent Vice President, David Kaplan, to whom I reported, is a brilliant guy who brings tremendous passion to whatever he does. He surrounds himself with capable people and relies on them to get the job done.

While the job required tremendous sacrifice and a lot of hard work, David always found a way to make us laugh and let us know he appreciated what we were doing. He could quickly assess a situation and come up with a strategy to make things better. He worked hard to collaborate with other departments to get his sales team and the company what they needed to win.

In reading Dave's comments, I'd be remiss if I, too, didn't thank the hundreds of people along the way who helped me get to where I've gotten— the hundreds of incredible sales people, managers, directors, customer service personnel, marketing, training, and the list goes on.

Thank God for giving me everything in my life: my family, my successes, my challenges, and for allowing me to come into contact with so many great people, like Dave Goldin, and my other mentors, who taught me so much.

Dave:

CINDY, MY WIFE OF 37 years, has been a stabilizing rock in my life's struggles. Pressures from work, relocating, and rearing two boys, Cindy always finds a way to continually smile though all of this. She is an amazing person. I am truly blessed. As the old saying goes; "Behind every successful man is an incredible woman." How true!

I had the good fortune of growing up in a stable home with a stay-at-home mom and a father with an incredible desire to be successful. This drive and desire was modeled for me every day. Jim & Carol Goldin have loved my brother Steve and me unconditionally. My dad modeled leadership, ethics, passion, and many other traits necessary to be successful. My mom was always there for my brother and me, carting us around to baseball, basketball, and football practice. Thanks Mom and Dad for your love and caring attitude.

Will is our oldest son and he is married to Caroline. They met during the time Will was getting his MBA from Emory University and Caroline was in medical school at Emory. They are expecting their first child, making Cindy and me grandparents for the first time.! Exciting times ahead.! We are very proud of Will and Caroline.

Michael is our youngest son and is married to Kristen. Both are graduates of Auburn University and have decided to make Auburn their home. Michael is very involved in a start-up company out of Atlanta, while Kristen continues her passion of teaching young girls how to ride, jump, and show horses. We are very proud of Michael and Kristen.

Cindy and I have been very blessed with our two sons!! As you can tell, I am very, very proud of my entire family. God has been good to us! I have too many business and personal friends to mention. However, a few come to mind that have made a tremendous impact on my life.

My brother, Steve Goldin, has an admirable entrepreneurial spirit. He is a very giving person with a super wife, Joni, and three incredible children (Courtney, Carson, and Aubree). Steve has worked for Fortune 500 companies over his career, including Coca-Cola, and has learned various business and leadership skills that make his company so successful today. He is a great friend and a man I am proud to call my brother.

Jim Robbins, a retired banker, is a friend that everyone dreams of having. He listens, coaches, counsels, and is always available to help out. I only wish there were more people like Jim Robbins on this earth. We would all benefit.

Mark Valentine is one of the most successful people at Johnson & Johnson. He was the first person I met when I assumed responsibility for training new hires. I knew within an hour he was going to be special.

Howard Miller, a fellow Auburn graduate, has been a close confidante for me over the years. Howard has served as president of several medical companies over his long and distinguished career. I believe that Howard possesses some of the most fundamental traits of a successful leader. He leads by example and is a hard worker. He is ethical, trust-worthy, a team builder, a tremendous judge of talent, and capable of molding that talent to perform at high levels.

Finally, I cannot go without mentioning a great friend I have in Chris Cunningham. What an inspiration he is to ALL with whom he comes into contact. He is the quintessential professional. Those who are fortunate enough to know Chris are very blessed people. I love him as if he were my brother.

I apologize to the hundreds of professionals and friends I have left out. Believe me, you have helped mold me and humble me. I have learned a lot from watching you. Thank you!

PREFACE

THE MOST IMPORTANT ASPECTS OF BEING A GREAT MANAGER
Jim Goldin, Retired Sr. Vice President
Atlanta GasLight Company

(Dave's father)

(My dad passed away back in 2016. Dean and I still wanted to leave Dad's writings to our book because in our opinion they are spot on. Love ya Dad and miss ya everyday !!!)

IT'S HARD FOR ME TO separate management and marketing, since most of my management experience was in the field of marketing. I began my career with Atlanta Gas Light as a salesman and retired as senior vice president, marketing. The irony was that I never really wanted to be a salesman. I didn't think I could sell. Most everyone else thought I could.

Before I get carried away with my thoughts, let me state my ideas on what I consider the most important aspects of being a manager. The first, and by far the most important, is INTEGRITY (moral soundness); the next is KNOWLEDGE (intelligence); the third is HARD WORK (with enthusiasm); BEING FAIR follows; and, finally FEEDBACK (two-way communications). We'll look at each one of these briefly.

Life is more than work and making money, even though without work we can't be successful and without money we can't support our families. We learn integrity from our parents and by going to church, synagogue, and other places of worship. Moral fiber means that your manager is not going to ask you to do anything that is dishonest or harmful to your customers. When your manager has integrity, he or she will always consider the consequences of what you are being asked to do. Without a lesson in "ethics," integrity comes from our beliefs in Judeo-Christian principals that are an important part of who we are and what we think. Each generation has an "event" that shaped their lives. Mine was World War II. That's the reason my generation is so patriotic. I remember the story of General MacArthur wanting to leave some word to his son, since he was away from his family so much. He wrote a letter, and told his wife to tell his son, "The word is integrity." This great general summed his thought to his only son with this letter.

The best managers know their product better than anyone else in the company. They are on the firing line, and their sales personnel constantly ask them about why their product is best. It takes intelligence to have superior knowledge, and that's why it's so important to study everything available to you.

I've never known a lazy manager who was successful. To be a good manager means you have to burn some midnight oil. This trait is contagious. Your salespeople will see your enthusiasm and will work tirelessly to make their quotas and not let you down. Remember, sales is a profession where failure is experienced every day. A salesperson knows with 100% certainty that he/she is going to fail with at least one call that day. He or she also knows that selling is the profession where success is so rewarding and so exhilarating the salesperson would rather be nowhere else. There is always victory in defeat. Before Roger Bannister broke the four-minute mile, he ran a thousand one-mile sprints at times over four minutes, but he kept on trying. Finally, one day in the summer of 1952, he crossed the finish line in three minutes and fifty-nine seconds. He worked hard; he had enthusiasm; and he became successful.

I know how difficult it is to be completely fair to all those under a manager's supervision. We all tend to like certain individuals more than others. It's human nature to be this way, but, in business, we must learn to treat everyone fairly. We all learn from experience, and a team will become much stronger when everyone works together. I'm reminded of a story I once told while making a speech in Boston. I used the expression "hanging around" meaning to loiter and compared it to "hang back," meaning to hesitate, "hang on," meaning to depend upon, "hang out," meaning to frequent, and "hang up," meaning to end a telephone conversation. But in Boston on that day, I meant "hang," to kill by suspending from a rope by the neck. This was the same meaning intended by Benjamin Franklin at the signing of the Declaration of Independence on July 4, 1776. He said, "We must all hang together, or assuredly we shall all hang separately." It's the same way in business—a team must find ways to hang together, or, better still, work together. The results will always be spectacular.

Feedback means for a manager to listen to his sales reps. It is amazing how much knowledge of the marketplace they have. Since the manager cannot be in the marketplace as much as his reps, he must depend on them for feedback. Many years ago, I heard of a textile manufacturing plant located in South Georgia. At one of its annual sales meetings, a young salesman asked the president what the company was going to do about the new "boxer shorts" that he was beginning to see being sold in his territory. The president told him it was nothing but a fad that would be gone soon. This plant had been producing long flannel underwear for men for more than 50 years, and it made the best in the industry.

At the next sales meeting one year later, the same young salesman told the president that more and more department stores were carrying the new boxer shorts. The president told the salesman that if he was unhappy with his job, he could move on to something else. In less than a year, the textile company was out of business.

Smart managers must always listen for feedback and relay it to management. This is how smart businesses keep being successful.

Remember, the best managers have integrity, are knowledgeable, work hard, always are fair, and listen for feedback.

WHAT IT TAKES TO BE A GREAT LEADER
Gerald Gould, President, Lehigh Acres Development Corp
(Dean's dad, who passed away in 2014)

Here are some of the traits needed to be a great leader:

1) Charisma – You must have the personality that inspires people to rally and succeed beyond the norm. You must have the ability to make people believe in you, the company, and your vision.

2) Communications Skills – Ability to transmit to all of your people the effect they have on the customer. For instance, if you own a hotel, the maid can destroy the image of the hotel. If you own a restaurant, the waiter can destroy the image of the restaurant. You must be able to transmit and communicate to your employees the impact they have on your business.

You must have an ability to communicate goals and a vision that everyone will strive for within the company, organization, or team.

3) Singularity of Purpose –Ability to get people to sacrifice or put the interest of the organization before your own interest.

The role of the chief executive (or managers) is that each must set goals for the company (or team) and single mindedly go after those goals. You must almost wear blinders and not get distracted by other opportunities. You must set your annual goals, but if you keep straying to other opportunities, not only will you fail to accomplish your annual goals, but you never get anything accomplished with the new ideas either. You'll be spread too thin.

4) Integrity – The reputation of you, the company, or your team must be that of living up to your commitments and promises. To meet those promises, a great CEO, president (or manager) must be willing to sacrifice in order to obtain those goals. A great leader must be willing to roll up his sleeves and do what it takes to help the team succeed.

INTRODUCTION

THANKS FOR READING OUR BOOK. For those of you who believe you know it all and are thinking, "Who are these two guys who think THEY have all the answers?" Just stop right there. We do not claim to believe our approach is the only approach to management. Our belief is this: No matter what you do in life, whether you are in management, sales, marketing, or basket weaving, there is always room for growth, and if you stop trying to learn, and you think you have it "wired," there is a good chance you will fail as time moves on.

We must all continue learning, growing, and, more important, remembering the basics. That is what happens to many great salespeople and many great managers; they quit doing the things that once made them great. For salespeople, it could be writing thank you notes or actually asking for the business and closing. For managers, it could be they quit providing feedback to their team through written and verbal communications.

At the beginning of every training camp while addressing some of the best football players of the day, Vince Lombardi, one of the greatest football coaches of all time, held up a football and said, "Gentlemen, this is a football." In basketball, John Wooden, who many think was the greatest coach of all time, would start out by teaching his players the correct way to wear socks to avoid blisters. What were their points? We've got to get back to basics, and then maybe we can learn a few new tricks.

You may not agree with every point in this book. That's OK. Let it go. Take a deep breath. But if you can learn just one or two new concepts or ideas, then mission accomplished. Some of you may manage from an approach of intimidation. In some companies that may work. We take a different approach. Different environment, different industries, different companies, and different products may require a variety of approaches, but we are confident there is tremendous value to be found in this book. Keep an open mind, and we are sure you will find some great techniques you can take back to your world.

For those of you just entering the management game, we ask, "So ya wanna be a manager; do ya?" Almost every sales representative, whether great or not-so-great, contemplates being a manager for various reasons, even if just for a minute. He or she may be bored. The person may hate his current manager and have visions of saving the day for fellow teammates. The person may just feel he or she can do a better job than a current manager. He or she may have converted almost all the possible business in a territory and believe that going into management is the way to keep a territory from sliding. The person could be running from something. The sales rep may have been brainwashed by the company's culture that management is THE career path the company wants all its reps to take. Maybe you have always known you wanted to lead, having been a college quarterback or team captain. Maybe you were the president of your sorority. Obviously, there are many reasons people go into management.

Before you go jumping into the fire, you've got to make sure that being a sales manager is truly the path you want to take, because if it isn't and you allow yourself to be pressured into the job, when you quit it will be bad for the company and certainly bad for you. It could also hurt your future career path if you chose to go back into sales after leading a team for only a short while.

We both agree that management is a very rewarding and fun job. Sure, there have been ups and downs for both of us, but for the most part, it has been great. Going into management, you may have a warped sense of what it is all about. Sometimes someone goes into sales for a large corporation because he or she wants to build a career and eventually be the president. Working your way up through the ranks is the right path to get there. The path at Johnson & Johnson was to be a top sales rep, become a sales trainer, and then possibly move into the corporate office working in marketing, sales admin, or sales training. After a year or so of that you then become a division manager, eventually moving up to region director. You might also become a marketing director, and, if you are really good, you might become a director of sales. From there, they could move you up to the title of VP of sales and marketing, and, at some point, you might become president of one of its 250-plus companies. Going into sales management is one path, and a great one it is. In order to do this, you needed to be flexible and willing to relocate.

There are those managers who love being the leader of a sales team in the trenches. They are frontline managers, who, for the most part, have their own autonomy, and they will always remain a sales manager with no aspirations to move up into "upper management." We have known great leaders like this. They do their own thing and produce winning teams, year after year. We have seen many sales reps go into management for a few years and realize their heart really lies in sales, or they just don't end up being very effective as a manager. They are most effective as a sales representative, and that's what they go back to do, sales, for the rest of their career. Sales is a very lucrative and noble career.

Whatever your motivation is to become a manager, just make sure you are doing it for the right reasons and that you are prepared to do a great job. Many top sales representatives believe that because they were great, they'll just get each of their reps to do things the way they do it, and that's how they'll achieve success as a manager. Unfortunately, you'll be setting yourself up for quick failure.

Other people have this strong desire to be "almighty" and powerful, finally reaching a position in which they can order others around. Through intimidation they believe they can achieve success. We believe this is another formula for failure. Others have this image of themselves becoming the "Great Motivator," and through sheer positive energy and cheerleading they will inspire all their reps to reach heights they never thought possible. Although this tactic of motivation can be part of your path to success, it is but one part of the entire formula of success as a mentor and leader.

Yes, management is a complex blend of art and science that can be taught, if you have an open mind and are willing to learn. There are those natural born leaders who are the exception. They just step into the role and from "the very get go" are good. But even those managers learn new ideas and methods along the way because as a manager, every day is new. You will encounter new situations and challenges that you never anticipated. There are other people who watch and learn from their managers throughout their sales career, learning the good things from the behavior of their great managers and what to avoid from their horrible managers. Throughout their career, they are actually developing the skills to become great managers. The reality is that there are very few managers who are great right out of the gate. The talents and traits can be learned quickly, but most people need to be taught a few things as well. Unfortunately, most companies don't have sales manager training, and, if they do, it often consists of a few days here and a few days there. It's unfortunate because many of these companies have tremendous sales training programs for their sales reps but somehow "miss the boat" on training managers.

We have had the opportunity to work and learn from the best. We were given great training throughout our careers and worked hard at self-improvement through reading books of this type. If you believe you don't need to learn anything more, you are missing out on the opportunity to reach even greater heights in your life and career. We have had the opportunity to not only work for several J&J companies and lead award-winning teams, but also build winning teams outside J&J.

---◆---

Dean

I came out to California to take over my first sales team and to date, have led a total of nine different teams in my management career. Many of the sales reps I managed initially suffered from the "California blues." Many of them believed that somehow our marketplace was more difficult than others, but I was and will always be unwilling to accept this mindset. At the same time, I also worked with some very positive thinking, can-do type salespeople who helped me change the mindset of the entire team. I am proud to say that I was able to take all six of the California teams from basically last place or almost last place to the top of the sales rankings. I was also able to instill some great ideas and programs within the national sales team I directed as well.

As a new manager, I probably suffered early on from the "I can motivate the entire team to want to be great" syndrome. What I soon learned was: 1) Everyone has their own motivations, 2) You can't manage or motivate everyone the same, and 3) There will be those who just don't care if they do well or not, and, thus, as a manager, it is your job to help them move on.

I have hired some phenomenal people who have gone on to leadership positions throughout the country. While you will NEVER see it all, I have encountered some incredible situations throughout my management career, as has Dave. I believe everything in life happens for a reason, and there is a lesson in each success and each failure that one encounters. I would not change one single step of my life or career, and I wish you the best in your management endeavor.

---◆---

Dave:

I was promoted to a division manager after selling for four years and being promoted to our home office, serving one year leading our sales training classes. At the ripe old age of 29, I thought I knew it all! Mistake after mistake taught me that I had a lot to learn. For example, my first few hires were disasters. I had not done my homework properly. I had not taken the advice of those with more experience; my gut told me I "thought" I had the right person. Was I ever wrong! After deciding to listen to those with more experience and to slow down the process of hiring, I improved. Remember, a rushed hire is usually a bad hire. Also, hiring someone no one knows or not using a referral system increases your odds of making a mistake. The absolute key to hiring is to minimize the odds of making a mistake. We'll discuss more of that later in the book. Once you build your team of winners, leading, coaching, and developing takes on a whole different light. You want to help them be successful. You have your stamp on them. They are a reflection of you. Your success depends on your team of winners.

———◆———

Management can be an incredibly rewarding endeavor if you enter for the right reasons with your eyes and your mind wide open. Both of us went back into sales for a short period, proving we still had "it," but returned to management because our passion was leading teams. It can be your passion as well. Just understand what management and leadership is all about and be open to learn from those who have been successful. The greatest management ideas, tools, and tactics you can learn are from other great managers. We hope to capture those tactics within this book.

You are not going to agree with every point in this book. In fact, if you are a president or VP of sales, don't throw the book away because you disagree with a point or two. Have your managers read it, and then use your next meeting as a chance to discuss the points you do agree with and the points you don't agree with and why.

If you study this book, it will give you a great head start and insight into what it takes to be a TOP sales manager. We believe we can provide you with unique insight you might not receive in a typical management book. The average manager usually doesn't have the opportunity to work with so many people in as many different situations as we have had the fortunate to experience. We are going to give you the real deal and share some great and some not-so-great experiences that will help you avoid some of the mistakes and capitalize on many of the successes that we have achieved.

1

MANAGEMENT ISN'T FOR EVERYONE

Nearly all men can stand adversity, but if you want to test a man's character, give him power.
- Abraham Lincoln, 16th U.S. president

PERSONALLY, WE BELIEVE THAT ONLY really good or great sales representatives should be managers, especially if a company is hiring from within. By the same token, not every great sales rep will make a great manager. For managers being promoted from within organizations, it is difficult for top sales rep to listen to the suggestions of someone who has only achieved average success as a sales rep themselves. Sometimes you'll see a marketing person asked to take over a sales team to gain experience on the sales side of the business. One idea, before allowing him to manage a sales team, is to ask that person to "carry a bag" for six months as a sales rep before taking over a sales team as manager.

There was once a general manager of a J&J division who did exactly that while he carried on his general manager duties. He was almost as high up in the organization as you can get, but he decided himself to take the step of carrying a sales bag. Granted, it was a carved-out territory around the New Jersey headquarters, but the bottom line was that he still got out there daily, toe to toe with the customers, and sold. Not only is it important to have sold prior to becoming a sales manager, but it is also important to know what sales management is all about.

———◆———

Dean:

One sales rep that comes to mind was second to none in his sales ability and consistently performed in the top 10%. He could still someday make a great manager if he chooses that path again, but it was bad timing for him. He was about to have a baby, and he didn't really understand the requirements and demands of being a sales manager. I had been promoted to Global Product Director and he was interested in backfilling my job. He asked me for my support for the job. Absolutely. He was a leader within my division, he knew the products better than anyone, he demonstrated maturity, and he had the respect of others on the team. He earned the right to interview for the job and get it for that matter.

I warned him, though, that while he was a great sales rep, it wouldn't be possible to get everyone to be just like him--that he might be frustrated by some of the ways people do things. During the interview process, I could tell his head just wasn't into it, but he felt obligated to interview and accept the job. He felt he had tapped out his territory from a market share standpoint, and he wanted to give management a try, which was not the best reason. He was very torn about taking the promotion.

I also warned him that for someone like him, it might be tough to handle the fact that not all his salespeople would live up to his expectations. He was one of the rare salespeople who basically did everything right. Not only was he a top salesperson, but he also did his paperwork and administrative duties perfectly and on time. He knew how to work with people inside the company to rally their support. He was an all-around salesperson and he still is. I advised him, "You have to understand that everyone is not going to be just like you. People are going to be late with expenses and monthly reports, and you are going to have to keep them in line. They are going to say stupid things in front of customers. They are going to make mistakes. While you can help people improve, you can coach them, you can fire them, but the one thing you can't do is make your nine people be just like you."

A few months into the job the frustration of being a manager mounted, and he realized that the timing was wrong. Luckily, he had not back filled his old position or territory. He decided he did not want to be a manager and went back to sales. He could have been and still could be a great manager, but that's not what he wanted.

Now the guy who replaced him should never have become a manager. While he was a decent representative, he lacked the tolerance and people skills to be a manager; hence, a year or so later, the company demoted him to being a representative. That doesn't mean he was a failure in life. It just means that some people have certain talents and certain weaknesses, and we must all strive to find our place in this world where we can most benefit others, our families, and ourselves. Management takes a certain type of person, and you and many others may not be well-suited for a management role. The message is to make sure you truly want to be a manager, that you are willing to obtain the skills to become a great manager, and to make sure the timing is right in your life to be a manager.

———◆———

Dave

My experience has taught me that many salespeople want to become sales leaders. However, only a few have the competencies it takes to become an effective manager. Traits such as leadership, coaching ability, recruiting and hiring the right people, putting someone on a performance plan for poor performance, empowering, and relationship building, not only with the representative but also with his/her family, are a few extremely important traits to have as a manager. Finally, courage to make decisions is a valuable trait needed to be an effective manager. Many managers do not possess the courage to make the tough decisions, especially about having to terminate a poor performer.

———◆———

While many of these traits can be developed, the problem is that many companies merely take a great sales representative and throw him into the fire as a manager, without any training. Every company should have a management development program, and this book can be a starting place. A management development program doesn't have to be an expensive initiative, but it will serve two purposes:

1) It will give the management trainee an insight as to what the job really entails.
2) It will allow the company to develop and assess the trainee's abilities to be or become a great manager.

Too many times a great sales representative who has served the company well for many years, is promoted into management, fails, and then fired or let go because there are no sales positions available. Yes, it is part of the risk you take in accepting a promotion, but it is also incumbent on the company to ensure you are qualified and prepared to lead. It is also incumbent on you, if management training is not provided, to read every possible book you can on how to lead and manage. Don't assume that just because you were the team captain in high school or you managed a coffee shop in college that you are ready to be a sales manager.

Many times, very good sales representatives approach the company about becoming sales managers. Deep down, you know as a manager the person isn't ready or will never be ready to be a manager, but instead of giving him honest feedback or coaching, the company just keeps overlooking the sales rep for management spots. Eventually, the person leaves the company in search of a company where a promotion is possible. You owe it to that person reporting to you to be honest! Coach him through your thought process. Find out his reasons for wanting to become a manager. Is it because his territory is "maxed out," and the sales rep is afraid his income will suffer? Is it because he believes that managers get special perks like stock options? Are those the right reasons to consider someone for a vital sales leadership position? As company leaders, it is incumbent on us to be honest and let people know where they stand and what it will take for them to become managers, rather than just pass them over and not provide feedback or coaching.

Again, the problem with many top sales reps wanting to get into management is they have a desire to have everyone perform or be just like them. They usually work extremely hard, their customers like them, they are very driven, they are self- motivated, and they are very accomplished as sales representatives. What you must realize as a manager is that the typical sales team has 15-20% top performers; 15-20% poor performers, and 60-70% average performers. Your goal as a manager should be to raise the performance level of your weakest links or get rid of them, and replace them with top performers. You'll want to raise the performance of the average workers, while retaining and continuing to motivate the top performers. The challenge is you can't do it all at once without massive turnover. In addition, **you can't go in and try to get everyone to be just like you.**

You must have time to assess your potential leaders and ensure they could actually succeed as managers. If a candidate has potential, you will need to develop and hone her/his skills. If promoting from within, the development of management skills can begin before promotion, laying the groundwork for a successful transition.

The bottom line is management isn't for everyone. Companies shouldn't set their best people up for failure. We need to train potential leaders and prepare them. Just as a manager always should want to fill his/her open territory with someone equal to or better than the rep who left, so should companies only want to fill their management spots with people who have the potential to be outstanding. If not, we need to develop them first to a point of being prepared or let them know they don't have the potential of becoming a manager in the organization.

2

GETTING STARTED

THE FIRST MONTH AND THE first 90 days are crucial for any new manager. Why do you think every recruiter tells you to write a 30-60-90-day plan for your interview? Why does almost every book on management discuss this issue? It's so important because the first 90 days will set the tone for your first year and your career. Get off on the wrong foot, and you may lose credibility with your sales team and upper management that could be difficult to overcome in the longer term.

During that first month, you are going to need to build credibility and trust with your team. Come in like hatchet man/woman, micromanager, or intimidator, and word will spread fast. You may not care about the feelings of the low-performing salespeople, but your best performers will mistrust you as well. First, get the "downloads" on each rep from your manager, the former manager, and anyone else that might have first-hand knowledge about each rep. Be careful not to form biases about the reps based on this information, but use it as a starting point for when you begin your own assessment. A good first step is to call each rep, individually, and spend at least an hour on the phone talking. Then, you need to immediately get out in the field and meet with each sales rep in person. You need to ask questions and listen. Find out where the person is at mentally. Hear what challenges each is facing, what frustrations each is feeling, and what opportunities each has. Do more listening than talking.

It is also important to look for low-hanging fruit or opportunities the rep is currently working on in which he/she needs your help. Achieve some early success, within the first month or two, that will help you build credibility with the team. Come into a new situation and start barking orders and intimidating people, and you lose the whole team fast. There will be performance issues you will need to address, but don't do it right out of the gate. You've got to get your top and even average performers "on your team" and moving forward before you start addressing your low-performing weak links. You will also need to put focus on any open territories you have in your division or region. Of course, you don't want to wait months to address any great opportunities to help the reps close business or fight off any major competitive threats.

The bottom line is you've got to work extremely hard during those first 90 days to "get the plane off the ground." If you sputter down the runway at 30 mph, you'll just run off into the bushes. You must get tremendous momentum going during that time to get the plane off the ground and headed for your end goal of a successful, winning team.

3

HIRE WINNERS TO BUILD A WINNING TEAM

Fire in the belly, drive, attitude, competitive, self-motivated, recognition oriented, money motivated, self-awareness: these are just a few traits of the real sales professionals.
- Dave Goldin

I LEARNED THE ABOVE TRAITS to look for when hiring, early on, from people like Dave and Rick Puleo. I believe these traits are more important than anything else you might find in a candidate. They are more important than experience or knowledge. - Dean Gould

We put this chapter right at the beginning, because without a doubt, this is one of the most important things you will do as a manager, not only for the company, but for your sake and sanity as well. Because of its importance, you must work extremely hard to find the right people. When you have an opening on your team, you must focus a large portion of your time on quickly and accurately filling the position. As they say, "Rush to hire, you'll be quick to fire," but you don't want to leave territories open too long. You should put great emphasis on hiring when the opportunity presents itself.

We can't stress this enough. Hiring will make or break your career as a manager. The number one reason we both have built and managed award-winning teams, often raising the teams from the bottom of the rankings to the top, has been our ability to identify and hire great people. It's the number one reason, but it's not the only reason. However, had we not hired great people, we would not have achieved the success that we did.

In order to maintain your sanity, you should not only hire great performing salespeople, but also hire people with whom you will enjoy working. There are those who will say that's ridiculous. Some sales directors or region directors may send you a resume of a top performer, but after interviewing the person, you find him/her to be difficult. Your mentor may try to force someone on you who you know will be a troublemaker. It doesn't matter what anyone says in this regard. Life is too short. When you have the opportunity to hire someone, go for a great salesperson and a great individual as well. You might have to put up with a lot from people you inherit on your team, but don't add to the challenges by hiring other problems.

Often companies are so focused on the sales representatives and their happiness that they somehow believe a manager should just deal with those people regardless of how difficult they might be. Too often companies overlook or undervalue the impact a great manager has on sales. The reality is that problem reps might not only be a "cancer" for your team, but their complaining and troublemaking can affect the entire sales force. Avoid them, don't hire them, and either ship up or ship out any other troublemakers already on your team.

You have to understand that salespeople can make your job the best job in the world or the worst job in the world. There is more to a sales representative than just a track record. You may have to work with a person for a long time. His/her attitude not only affects your life and enjoyment, but also affects the life and enjoyment of teammates, customers, and those who work in support roles. We have managed and observed some of the greatest sales reps in the world from a performance standpoint. But sometimes some of those same sales reps bothered, annoyed, and angered everyone around them. There comes a point when the attitude of I, me, me, me, Mr. Numero Uno doesn't outweigh the negative brought to an organization. A selfish individual attitude can infect the whole team, causing fragmentation and canceling out any positive that person's sales performance brings. The balance of confidence without ego is a key for long-term success.

Don't take the attitude of "I can manage anyone," or "You've got to let the wild stallions run," or "You've got to give a workhorse some slack." All those sayings are great in theory, but only up to a point. The same holds true for everyone in an organization--including managers. No one individual is more important than the team as a whole. So, hire great people with great track records and great attitudes. Let the stallions run, but unmanageable crazy horses should be set free.

The other challenge you may face in an open territory is that you may not find the right person for a month or two, and you many begin to panic. First, don't set your standards so high they are unrealistic. Yes, you want people to be great with top track records, but you've also got to be realistic. People suffer from this in their personal lives, searching for the perfect man or woman, and they end up still single when they are older. You've got to set high standards but realize that very few candidates are going to be all-around 10s. In addition, in a city like Atlanta or Los Angeles, with thousands of people from which to choose, you should be able to find someone who is a "10," but you may have challenges in Savannah or Bakersfield. You can't wait forever for a "10" in these cities when there is an 8 or 9 ready to go. Remember, if the applicant has the drive and passion but not the perfect experience, you may have a diamond in the rough that you can potentially turn into a 10.

Depending on how strong your company is or how tough it is to find great candidates in a market, you may have to settle for an 8 or 9. Just don't settle for a 7 or below, because nine out of 10 times, the person will remain a 7 or below. Always remember that. You can motivate and coach a 7 to perform as an 8 temporarily, but it will be a constant struggle to keep the rep performing at that level. Better to hire the person with the winning attitude who will strive to be at that top level than constantly pushing him/her to perform at that level. Your life will be so much easier, and you can use that energy to focus on other average salespeople whom you didn't hire. If you set unobtainable standards for your situation, recruiters may give up and quit looking. In addition, recruiters are paid when your hire someone, so they will often try to sell someone to you. YOU need to understand your marketplace and the position of your company, and YOU need to decide when someone is the right fit, not the recruiter.

Dean:

If you want your job to be as easy and simple as possible, when you must hire people, only hire great people. The few times I have hired the wrong people, it made things so much more difficult. One of the easiest, most fun years I had in management was a year that I was able to hire four new people to complement a few great tenured reps. I had the chance to upgrade the team. I was lucky to hire four outstanding salespeople, and, thus, my entire team was "on fire." I had eight great people and a strong mixture of tenured experience and young enthusiasm. We blew the doors off and had several people win award trips to Hawaii. It was just fun. The entire year was a pleasure and very rewarding.

———◆———

Dave:

I enjoy hiring! The process of meeting first with a candidate and formulating if this person would fit in was intriguing. I looked for winners! How do you know when you've got one? That's the hard part and why successful leaders are successful and average managers/leaders are average. As you read through this book, words like passion, drive, recognition, "fire in the belly," competitive spirit, and attitude, are all traits of people I wanted on my team. Some of this was gut instinct. A lot of putting a team together is finding someone you like during the interview process and then challenging him/her. Make sure you like the person with each progressive interview more than you did the previous interview. Set the expectations HIGH. Inspect what you expect!

4

WINNERS COME IN MANY SHAPES AND SIZES

If each of us hires people who are smaller than we are, we shall become a company of dwarfs. But if each of us hires people who are bigger than we are, we shall become a company of giants.

- David Ogilvy, father of advertising

DON'T MAKE THE MISTAKE OF trying to hire everyone who is just like you. Don't get the preconceived notion that a "winner" looks or acts a certain way, and if the person doesn't fit that mold, he/she must not be a winner.

Having a winning attitude comes from within. It is an inner drive, and how that inner drive is expressed on the outside varies from person to person. There are some great salespeople who are the life of the party. Everyone loves being around them. They are incredibly charismatic.

However, sometimes there are great salespeople who are much more reserved and tactical. They win through challenging the thinking of customers, through hard work, honesty, integrity, going the extra mile, and caring about their customers. Just be careful not to overlook a great candidate because the person doesn't don't fit the cookie-cutter mold you have created in your mind.

Dean:

Recently, I asked one of the most successful recruiters in the industry if she personally interviewed each candidate face to face. Her response was, "I quit interviewing candidates face to face when I met some of the other recruiter's candidates who managers hired. I took a look around at how overweight and unattractive some of the managers are out there. It's a waste of time." I guess her point is, "Beauty is in the eye of the beholder." Successful salespeople come in many shapes and sizes. Oh sure, in the short term, an attractive person will get the attention of customers, and it will open doors, but will they be able to get and keep the business? If she is a great sales person; a challenger; and is also a hard worker and driven; she will!

Luckily, I've made mostly incredible hires, but the two times I struck out, I probably knew it during the interview. Sometimes you want so badly for someone to work out. You like the person and enjoy his/her personality, and maybe too much time has gone by with your territory open. Looking back, your gut was telling you the person didn't truly have the passion, image, and drive, but you still pulled the trigger and made the mistake.

Early in my career, I had a territory that was next to impossible to fill. I must have interviewed every candidate in the area. Late in the process, I met one candidate who had a tremendous personality. He was witty, upbeat, seemed to know everyone, and said all the right things. But there was something fishy about his track record, and I couldn't seem to get any good references. I went against my gut and better judgment and hired him. It became apparent pretty quickly that he was just a bag of hot air. He was his own best fan, and he never amounted to anything. He turned out to be a whiner, a gossiper, a name dropper, and a troublemaker. He had every excuse in the book as to why he couldn't sell any products. If I had taken my time, investigated his background a little more, and followed my gut, I wouldn't have made that mistake. It took us too long to get rid of him, and, luckily, he didn't pull the team down too much. I'm happy that was a rare occurrence during my career.

The people I've hired have come from wide, diverse backgrounds, and they came in all shapes and sizes. I tried to focus on what was inside and less on the outside--a philosophy that served me well.

———◆———

Dave:

Having the privilege to hire many salespeople over the years, the most successful people had a tremendous drive to be successful. Probably one of my BEST hires was made in 2002. I had an open territory after the previous representative was let go. So, as always, I started asking around if anyone knew a superstar who could fill this very important territory. Many came forward with resumes, friends, etc. The one resume that caught my eye was from a young man who had ZERO background in our business. However, in his objective statement at the top of his resume, he stated, "An intense desire to be the best," "An intense desire to be recognized," and, "An intense desire to get into our field of medical device sales."

After checking him out and talking with the person who had referred him to me, I agreed to meet with him. He is a nice-looking young man, not very personable at first, very business-like, hard to get to know in a first interview. However, there was something about him that just stood out! He had a burning desire, had a fantastic work ethic based on referrals, and was very recognition-oriented and money-motivated. However, I just couldn't get beyond the fact that I was having a hard time getting to know him. If I'm having a tough time, what are our customers going to feel when this guy walks in the door and introduces himself as our new company representative?

I sent him out on two separate field visits with two different representatives whom I trusted completely. Both were blown away! I asked, "What made him a candidate whom I should really consider?" The answer that came back astonished me. "His ability to build relationships quickly with our customers is fantastic." He was very prepared and asked many well thought-out questions to our customers, which they respected. He endeared our customers to him because he cared so much about learning! In our day-to-day business of calling on physicians, a sales rep does not need the personality of a Jay Leno.

At the end of some serious soul-searching, I offered this young man a position. He and his wife wrote me thank you notes for giving him this opportunity! Now when does that ever happen? Over the four or five years I managed him, he hit his forecast every year, was awarded our presidents club trip every year, was a field sales trainer, and was a guy I pointed to and used to teach other managers about hiring. He was not our typical hire, but he had the drive, hunger, desire, motivation, work ethic, attitude, curiosity, and humility, to become well respected by ALL of his customers and our company's sales organization. Now the company has to work extra hard to keep him because all of its competitors want to hire him.

What matters most in a candidate is how much heart he/she has and how much drive, passion, and ambition the person possesses. This is what separates the long- term winners from the long-term losers. You can't replace these traits, no matter someone's background or experience. Take a look at the people who walk up on stage at your next awards banquet. You'll see that they don't fit a certain mold.

Don't hire based on someone's outside appearance over what is going on inside the person's heart. Things about your products, industry, and customers you can always teach, but you can't teach someone to have heart, passion, and drive. Get very good at flushing out these important characteristics. Many people try to fake it, so be careful. Many people get good at answering interview questions the way you want to hear them answered. A good interviewer will pick up on that. Drill down. Get multiple examples of their success.

So many managers aren't interested in people who don't fit in the perfect mold. Sometimes, it's tough to fill territories so **be careful not to overlook a diamond in the rough.** There isn't anything wrong with trying to keep to a basic formula in your hiring, but be careful you don't pass on a great candidate because they don't fit perfectly in your mold.

5

HIRING EXPERIENCE: IS IT ALWAYS NECESSARY?

Good people do good work, lousy people don't.
- Mike Dunkerley

THIS DISCUSSION IS IMPORTANT ENOUGH to give its own chapter. Remember, drive and enthusiasm always win out over experience in the long run. Sometimes you'll need veterans. Just don't burden yourself with average veterans; your team will remain average. If your company wants an immediate impact, you may need some veterans who can go out and turn old relationships fast. Be careful, though. Average veterans can only "turn" so much business. If upper management is more patient and will let you build your team, try to hire all A players regardless of tenure. It's a balancing act. If you don't have a lot of time and you just can't seem to uncover A players with experience, then you may have to hire A players without experience and teach them how to succeed with your company's products. What do you do if YOU don't have the experience with those products to teach them? You may need to have others within the company teach them.

There are many factors to consider when deciding whether to hire experience or not. Are there noncompete laws that can be upheld in your state that will prevent you from hiring the competition? Even if you manage in a state like California, will your company have the willingness to stand behind a competitive rep that comes to your team? Many won't. They'd rather not spend the legal fees if the competition comes after them.

Are you building a team from scratch? When in doubt, hire all A players, regardless of experience, and bite the bullet. Try and get a mix of experience and non-experience, but realize that the company may not have the time, patience, or funding to wait for results. It can be a tough decision, but if you focus on the issues, the answers will come. One good approach is to have discussions with your VP or director and see what he/she suggests. That way, others will buy into whatever decision you make, and they will be supportive. For instance, suppose you and your manager agree that hiring A players is extremely important. He/she sees you've tried to find a candidate with experience, but you can't find a seasoned A player. When you eventually hire fewer experienced A players, upper management will fight for you if the turnaround doesn't happen quite as fast as the company would like.

Dean:

Hiring people without experience or the typical background in your industry is going to take courage. Your mentor may not approve. I've watched average managers my entire career hire experience only to have their teams stay in the middle of the pack. They believe that these people will turn business over quickly, but if they are average to begin with, the benefits will be short-lived and limited. I've seen new reps, without specific experience and relationships, turn business just as fast, or faster, then people with specific experience. Why? Because they had more drive and they figure out a way to get in to see customers and close business. Sure, if you can find an A player who has the experience and relationships, absolutely hire them. Just make sure they are A players, because B or C players will most probably always remain B or C players, and your team's level of performance will never rise. You may be able to get a C player to perform at a B level for a period, but, usually, they will fall back to their C-level ways regardless of how good a coach you are.

One of my best hires had no experience selling to cardiovascular surgeons, but he did have a track record of strong success and converting lots of business fast. While some of the other managers in our organization were focused on cardiovascular experience, I was focused on hiring A+ players. This rep came on board, and, from Day One, he tore it up. He ended up rookie and sales rep of the year and helped me win region manager of the year, along with some other strong performances on the team.

Dave:

My 35+ years of management has taught me many things. One of the most important things is dealt with in this chapter. Winner over experience? No-brainer!!

My strong suggestion to each of you is to hire winners with the attributes that we have been describing. I would rather spend more time and potentially lose immediate business opportunities for the long-term gain of hiring someone I feel confident will more than make up the loss in the long run. Bottom line: Do not ever hire for the short-term and think a person with "experience in your field" is the answer. I believe this is a recipe for failure. If you are the courageous leader, I would want you to stand up and do the right thing. Hire the person you believe a year from now is going to excel. Usually it's the A+ player over the experience. Why? Simple. The winner has the successful traits. The experienced person could have developed many bad habits over the years. If you don't believe me, just ask anyone who hires people. Ask him/her this question: "Would you rather hire someone who already knows our business and throw the person out there with a forecast and let them go, OR would you rather hire someone with no understanding of your business but has the drive, desire, attitude, work ethic, and curiosity to learn--a person that your organization can mold?"

───◆───

Hiring all seasoned veterans for the short term or hiring a mixture of seasoned veterans and young guns depends on the situation. Is the company a start-up? You may need relationships to jump start sales. Is the company more mature? A mixture should work. Make sure you understand what upper management expects. Do they want short-term, immediate results, or do they want you to build a team for long-term sustained growth? Will the board or VP of Sales wait for you to build a long term winning team or do they want results NOW?

As you ponder this study, there are several things to consider.

1) If there is no patience to allow non-seasoned rooked to get started, you could be out of a job.

2) Again, with a start-up, seasoned veterans with relationships can potentially, but not necessarily, get you sales. Are they A player veterans?

3) If you go with the seasoned, experienced veterans, realize that it is not easy to get rid of them if they are just barely getting the job done. If you have a bunch of C+ players that just barely get past forecast each year, you will have to judge them based on the overall performance nationally versus hitting forecast.

There are a lot of questions you must ask when hiring but, in most situations, if you have a B- or C+ player with lots of experience and an A+ player with limited experience, go with the A player. Of course, your ultimate goal is to find the A+ player with experience.

> *First-rate people hire first-rate people; second-rate people hire third-rate people.*
> *- Leo Rosten*

6

THE STEPS TO TAKE TO HIRE WINNERS

To me, a winner is someone who recognizes his God-given talents, works his tail off to develop them into skills, and uses those skills to accomplish his goals. Even when I lost, I learned what my weakness were, and I went out the next day to turn those weaknesses into strengths.
- Larry Bird, the great Boston Celtic

WHEN YOU HAVE AN OPENING, the steps to take immediately are as follows:

1) **Make the hiring** of your new candidate **a top priority**. The longer the territory stays open, the more time it will take away from your being able to bring on new business with your other sales reps, and the more risk you'll have of losing business.

---◆---

Dean:

I am always amazed at how long it takes some managers to even begin the interview process when they have an opening. Then they'll take months to actually pull the trigger and fill it. It is rumored that one medical device company has a policy that requires managers to interview 40 people before they hire someone. Based on the performance of that company and watching its interview process, it seems to be true. I think the company believes that the policy results in hiring the best people. It takes so long, though, that by the time the manager gets around to interviewing the 40 people, some great salespeople who were interested in the job have either taken other jobs, or they are so frustrated that their interest in the company is gone. One recruiter told me that he lets all the other recruiters fight it out in the early rounds and then comes in at the end and places the first few candidates he sends. I say, focus on finding an A player, and when you find them, hire them.

———◆———

2) Try to **get one of your other sales reps to help cover** the open territory. Hopefully your company will compensate the other rep for her/his time. Otherwise, it is very difficult to get salespeople, who are being held accountable to their forecast and trying to put food on their family's table, to get them to spend time away from their territory to cover another territory. This is especially true when they don't make additional money for working that territory and it doesn't count toward their forecast.

Yes, sometimes you end up paying them for doing nothing and you want to hold them accountable. It is your job to make sure they are actually working the open territory. Sometimes they just never quite get into the other territory, but they'll tell you they've been working like dogs and have earned every penny of the extra stipend. Just **weigh the situation**, because every situation is different. You may be up to your ears in alligators and don't have a lot of time to devote to the empty territory, so you may be forced to get another salesperson to cover, but keep in mind that this spreads that person thin, and he/she will possibly become less effective in their own territory.

3) **Begin networking with people you know in the industry to find a great candidate.** Some managers never use recruiters. They are so well connected in the industry and know so many people that they prefer to find their own candidates. If you are new, don't have a lot of contacts outside your company, or you just don't have the time, contact a great recruiter.

4) **Contact your number one recruiter** and give that person a two-week head start to find great candidates. (We will discuss working with recruiters in the next chapter). Some managers like to open things up to three or four recruiters at a time. Some open it up to anyone who calls. This builds no loyalty, and you won't get much focus out of any of them. Remember: Your commitment to the

recruiter will equal his/her commitment to you. Call every recruiter in the book, and you will get about 1/10 effort from each. It is an absolute fact. Time is money. If a recruiter has a 1/10 chance of getting someone hired or can work on another job order in which he/she has an exclusive, which one would you work on? I know recruiters will think a two-week head start is not enough but today, the pressure is high and time is short.

5) **Contact other managers and sales representatives** within the company and outside the company to see if anyone knows any great candidates. Many companies offer an incentive for their representatives to bring good candidates forward, but be careful. Whenever you offer salespeople money, you could get a flood of unqualified candidates.

———◆———

Dean:

Other managers in the industry are great resources for great sales reps. The minute I had an opening, I would start calling other non-competitive managers in the industry with whom I was friends, and in my area, to see if they knew of someone. At the same time, I called my best recruiter and get him started as well. Remember, everything in life is about giving so when those managers or recruiters call to get your help, it's best to take a few minutes, think about it, and see if you can help them out.

———◆———

6) **Call all the large customers**, within the territory and let them know of the departure of the former rep if you think they may be unaware the person left. Also **let them know that you are there for them** and will get in there at any point to take care of any issues. Sometimes, if you are having a difficult time finding good people, ask your good customers if they know of great salespeople whom they would like to see in the job. Let them know upfront that the salesperson needs to have at least two years of sales experience, a degree, and a great track record of success (or whatever your requirements are). In your industry, you may or may not require a degree, and you may or may not require experience in your industry.

Be careful, because it could be a double-edged sword. They may want the job themselves and may be unqualified. They may also be upset if you don't hire someone they recommend. Many times, the person a customer thinks is a great rep isn't always who you might think is a great rep.

———◆———

Dean:

I inherited a sales rep working for me who was a great, great guy. Everyone loved him, including the customers. He had more product knowledge in his left pinkie than most other representatives had altogether. The problem was that he never, ever asked for business. His idea of sales was dropping samples off and hoping the customers liked the product. Usually, nine out of ten times they never used the samples. The lab manager didn't want the doctors to convert. If I depended on the customers for recommendations on this guy, many would say they loved him. He was NOT a salesman, and so that's an example as to when a customer recommendation isn't good for hiring a great sales rep.

———◆———

7) Make it a point to **get into the accounts where you have large amounts of business**, personally, and go see the customers. They appreciate it, and often you can pull products out of the bag. Why not? You're a sales manager. Hopefully you still remember how to sell, and it always impresses the other salespeople in your team to know that you "still have it." If you have newly launched products, you must absolutely be sure to let the customers know about them. If too much time passes, they'll wonder why they didn't know about them, and they'll be disappointed.

8) **Consider asking a marketing person, sales admin, and/or customer service to help you keep in touch with customers** and maintain business. Often the marketing people would love an excuse to get out of their offices and go see customers. This is another reason to get along with everyone inside a company. You just never know when you will need their help. It's a good idea to get along with almost everyone in this world, because people will rally on your behalf if you treat them with respect and help them.

9) If your number one recruiter doesn't begin producing some decent leads **after two weeks, open it up to your number two recruiter**. After three weeks, you might open it up to several recruiters. No recruiter likes this strategy, but the reality is that recruiters have different relationships with different reps, and the first recruiter may not know that perfect candidate for whom you are looking. If your best recruiter doesn't produce, it may just mean that he doesn't have the right candidates for that search. Don't give up on him or her. It may just be bad timing. You built your loyalty with the recruiter for a reason, but after two or three weeks, you've got to get that train out of the station. Most great recruiters will find you at least a few good candidates within the first week. Some belong to national networks and can post the job, anonymously, out to the group and get even more candidates.

10) **Make sure your recruiters and other sales representatives on your team clearly understand the criteria you look for in a sales representative**, otherwise, they will waste a lot of your time. Often sales representatives are approached by their customers for jobs with the company, and they just pass them on to you, putting you in the uncomfortable position. If they understand your criteria, they can repeat it to the customer, which usually shuts down the discussion. For instance, most advanced medical sales jobs require 4+ years of device sales experience. A nurse just doesn't have that background but might be able to join another company as a nurse educator, etc.

11) **Don't allow scheduling conflicts to allow you to pass on a superior candidate**. So many managers decide: I'm interviewing on Wednesday, and if the rep can't make it, I'm moving forward. Unfortunately, they move forward without the best candidate. Remember, this is one of the most important decisions you will make as a manager. Be flexible!

HERE ARE SOME SUGGESTED CRITERIA FOR YOUR SEARCH:

1) Very strong, VERIFIABLE track record. Top 10% throughout career. Award- winning resume: president's club, award trips, sales rep of the year.

2) At least two years of sales experience. (unless your job is entry level). No job hoppers. If someone has bounced every 2 years, even if the person has great reasons, there is a high probability he/she will bounce again. If the applicant wants the job for the money alone, move on. If you hire someone in those circumstances, more than likely you will lose the person to the next company that pays more. It's always good to hire someone who is going to get a pay raise by coming with your company. If someone was making $120k and can make $150k with your company, that's a good fit.

3) A Challenger. A great book to read is *THE CHALLENGER SALE*. A challenger is someone who can change the mindset or paradigm of a customer and insure their products are a part of that change.

4) Great personality that customers will like. Fun to be around and can build instant rapport with customers.

5) Team player. Someone who cares about others and not just about himself.

6) Great references and be sure to check them! Take the time. It will save you a tremendous amount of time avoiding a bad hire. Don't rely on others, like your recruiter or HR to check references. Check them yourselves.

7) Professional.

8) Attitude . . . is the multiplier!! A person with a great attitude will cancel out any lack of experience…Have we made that point yet?

9) Good person. Ethical.

Know this: Everything can't be perfect while interviewing. Be flexible. Wait for the great candidates. Minimize the risks of hiring the wrong candidate.

The decisions you make on these people will be what sets the tone for your management career. Sometimes, the company or your manager may try to pressure you to hire someone they recommend because 1) He or she is friend, 2) The person worked with them at another company, and 3) The applicant is the relative of a customer. You owe it to yourself to always hire the best candidate. In the short run, it may be difficult or painful, but, in the long run, you are going to make your life easier. If, in your heart of hearts, you know you have someone much better than their candidate, you must make the better decision. Remember, when their candidates don't do well, and your division isn't hitting forecast, they won't let you use the excuse that THEY made you hire their candidate. They will merely say, "We asked you to look at him/ her; we didn't tell you to hire the person."

People in higher places don't necessarily have better hiring skills than you. You know what a winner looks like, and they are the people you need to hire. You need to hire total winners. Average people will only keep your division average. Believe it or not, you will only be able to motivate average people to perform slightly better for maybe a year, but average people almost always fall back to being average. You may think you can inspire average people to change their lives and decide to be a high-charging, Top 10% salesperson, but this rarely happens. It doesn't matter how great a manager you are.

Also, don't always look for someone exactly like you because you may not find that person. If you do, great, just know that the chances of finding someone just like you are slim, and it could take you a year to find that person. Be sure to hire someone who can perform in the TOP 10%.

Your six to 12 reps are your world and a big part of your life. Hire someone who is a pain in the rear, and he/she can make your life miserable. Just because reps like to call you a lot and brainstorm doesn't make them a pain. That just means they are engaged. Some great reps love to call their managers daily and brainstorm. If you love to manage, then you will love to hear from these highly-charged, motivated people. When we are talking about troublemakers, these are people who your gut tells you they are unreasonable, self-center, psycho, or just overly difficult. Don't do it. Don't hire them. Your happiness is just as important as anyone else's happiness. Some reps you inherit may already be problems, so don't hire more problems.

Finally, let others in your organization interview the final candidates. Get other people's opinions. If you trust their judgment, they can provide good feedback. But at the end of the day, the decision is yours.

———◆———

Dean:

Having been a recruiter for two years, it has been truly amazing to watch the horrible people managers hire and to watch the horrible hiring practices. This is such an important part of being a top manager, but yet so many fail or remain average. There are many strategies and tactics, but so many of them are flawed. We've outlined the way to hire winners. Incorporate them, and you'll hire great people.

> *Here lies a man who knew how to enlist the service of better men than him.*
> *- Tombstone of Andrew Carnegie*

7

TIME KILLS DEALS

Always rush to hire, but never hire in a rush until the Top Dog walks in the room.

- Dave Goldin

NEVER RUSH TO HIRE BECAUSE often you will hire the wrong person. However, that doesn't mean you should drag your feet to begin the process. In addition, when you do find the right person, don't waste time getting the person on board. Time kills deals is an adage that applies to all business. For the most part, in hiring, it's a bad thing. Many great salespeople are lost to other companies because of managerial incompetence and the bureaucracy of companies. When you find a great candidate, that A+ player, get him/her through the system and GET THE PERSON HIRED!

As a manager, when you have a territory open, drop most everything else you are doing and focus your energy on filling that position. If you don't, the ramifications for dragging your feet are:

1) You will spend a tremendous amount of time covering customer phone calls, emergencies, customer service issues, and everything else that starts coming your way as a manager. Empty territories are tremendous TIME KILLERS.

2) There is no way that you can cover that territory on a part-time basis and still be an effective manager to the other reps and territories. Eventually, the business will start to slide.

3) The longer the territory is empty, the more chance competitors have to convince the customers that "it is their turn" and start converting business.

4) The customers start to forget about the company because the sales representative was really the face of the company.

5) Hiring great people is sometimes about recruiting great people, and if you drag your feet, the recruiters get frustrated and move on to other job orders. Even worse, the great candidates who may have been contacted by you may eventually take other jobs. Time kills deals.

The list goes on and on. So, when you have an opening, focus all of your attention on finding the best candidate fast. If you ask most successful, award-winning managers what was the most important thing they did to rise to success, most will reply that their ability to hire great people was the Number 1 thing, but **not the only thing**.

Sometimes, though, it will be difficult. Life happens as we are planning. The VP of sales starts asking for a special report. Customer service wants all the consignment inventory reports completed and rolled up. A representative calls you to go meet with a huge customer because he/she is about to lose a million-dollar deal. Rather than staying focused on hiring that great candidate, you get sidetracked and allow this priority to slip down the list. For new managers, there is the fear of making a hiring mistake, so they drag their feet. If you are new and you find a great candidate, there's nothing wrong with having a SUCCESSFUL, tenured manager interview the person also. Many companies today require three or four people to interview a candidate to help weed out bad hires. Get the process moving by finding great candidates and get the process started.

So many times, recruiters will send managers perfect candidates—studs, studettes. hunters, killers, Top 10%'ers—and the managers drag their feet. After a few weeks, the awesome candidates take other jobs or get disillusioned about your company and about you because of the stop-and-go. Sometimes companies will give a manager approval to hire someone or to create an expansion territory. After he/she has spent a lot of time recruiting, the company puts a hold on the opening. Then three weeks later companies release the approval to hire someone again. By now three great candidates are gone or uninterested. TIME KILLS DEALS.

8
HOW TO INTERVIEW

A manager asked a candidate to bring several copies of his resume and three references. He called back an hour before the interview and asked to reschedule, saying his references couldn't come with him to the interview.

LOCATION: AS FAR AS WHERE to interview people, that is a personal preference. Some people interview in hotel lobbies, some in restaurants, and some in conference rooms. Many people say, "You should never interview in a restaurant," but it works for many people. Restaurants tend to be distracting, which can be a good test for the candidate. When selling, is the environment always perfect? It can also cause people to relax and let down their guard. People can end up saying the craziest things in a relaxed setting. It can help you find out who they really are.

Some people like to rent out a conference room in a hotel and put people under the hot lights. They make it a real *DRAGNET* experience. They have a very structured line of questions and drill the candidates. Some like to use a more conversational interview—very relaxed, very casual. Whatever works for you is the best path. You can go with a relaxed first interview, then hit candidates with a structured, tougher second interview, or you can give them a structured tough interview, followed by a more relaxed "get to know you better" second. Some might choose to be relaxed during both or drill people back to back.

Dean:

When I'm filling a position, I like to take complete control of the process. I'll have the recruiter send me the candidates, and that's the last help I need from the recruiter until the end. Some managers like to have the recruiter act like a secretary, or go between, setting up the interviews, having them fill out forms and online questionnaires. I do all that. I don't have time for the phone tags and other time wasters. I don't rely on anyone to set my appointments. If you wait for others to get things done, a month can go by, but a good recruiter is incentivized to keep things moving.

The first thing I do when I get a handful of good candidates is to do a 10- or 15-minute phone screen with each. I tell the recruiter to let them know I'll be calling. I don't set an appointment to call them—I just call. If they can't collect their thoughts and sound presentable off the cuff, what are they going to do when they run into a customer in an elevator or in the parking lot? If they are great reps, they know what they've accomplished in their lives. I don't make it too tough on the phone screen. I just want to get through some of the basic resume "stuff" so I can ask them more in-depth questions in person. I also like to weed out people I think are less than truthful or overstate the truth on their resumes. For instance, if someone says on the resume that he/she was rookie of the year, I'll ask, "How many rookies were in your class?" If there were two, well that's OK. But if there were 20, then that is quite an accomplishment. If I ask people what their ranking was, and job after job they say the company didn't have rankings, that raises questions.

If they say on their resume that they were top 10%, then I ask, "How many people were in your sales force. If there were 200, then I ask, "Were you Number 20 or Number 10?" I try to determine if they are BSing on their resume or if they really did the things they say. If they pass the phone screen, I'll set up a time to meet with them in person. I'll pick a day in the near future and see four to six people. If I'm not finding great candidates in the first week, but I did find one standout, I might plan to meet him/her between travel or sales calls with my reps during the next few days. I'm flexible because I want to get the right person hired but hired fairly fast. I want to keep things moving. Once I identify the right candidate, then I take responsibility to get the person through the process. I work with HR to get the candidate lined up with the internal folks who need to see him/her, or I'll do it myself. If people are on vacation, then I set up those who are available. There's no time to wait two weeks for one person to get back from vacation to get this person through the process. Unless it is absolutely necessary to have that one candidate meet with certain people, I work with whoever is available to see the person ASAP. There are no reasons why a great candidate can't make it back to the home office, interview, and have background checks completed within a two-week period. If you wait for other people, it could take three months to have someone hired and processed. No one will have the sense of urgency you will have.

Time per interview: How should the interview process go? It depends on how many interviews you plan to conduct. Two or three is usually the norm. The initial interview may be a "get to know you" interview." If you line up five or six candidates back to back in one-hour intervals, you really only have time to briefly go through their resumes during that first round, to determine who should return for a second interview.

Phone Interviews: Some managers don't like to do phone interviews, but we feel they can be a tremendous time-saver. Because most recruiters don't properly screen candidates, 10 minutes on the phone can save you 30 minutes to an hour of valuable face-to-face time. This is not to say that you shouldn't give someone the benefit of the doubt, but phone screens can eliminate people who are not even close. In addition, you can get some basic information on the phone and skip that part during the live interview. During the phone interview, go through the candidate's resume from the bottom to the top.

Ask them their GPA. Have them tell you about anything they may be proud of that isn't on their resume. If it is an entry-level sales job, have them tell you about their accomplishments in high school and college. Look for a pattern of success throughout their lives. Look for gaps between jobs. When someone only puts years on their resumes without the months, it is an immediate red flag they are hiding gaps. Gaps may NOT be a deal killer. If someone works long enough, the person will probably have a gap at some time, but you need to dig deeper to find out the reasons for gaps. There are often gaps between college and someone's first job.

What did they do during that time? Did they travel? Were they looking for a job? How about the other gaps? Did they just quit a job before they had another? Did they have a problem with their manager? During the background checks, you can often uncover the "real deal" as to why someone left a job.

It's interesting to note that many companies try to come up with formulas, tests, personality traits, lists of attributes or profiles, huge lists of questions, and multiple interviews with multiple people in order to help managers hire the right people.

These techniques aren't necessarily wrong and can be useful. If you want to use the questionnaires and checklists, go for it. It can't hurt, especially if you are a new manager. You may need the structure as a guide in order to help ensure you hire the right people.

9

WHAT TO LOOK FOR IN A GREAT SALES REP

Great people are just ordinary people with an extraordinary amount of determination.
- Garner Dunkerly, senior. founder, Ennis Business Forms

THESE TRAITS MAY SIMPLIFY THE process:

1) Burning desire to succeed. Passion

2) Enthusiasm

3) At least two years of sales experience

4) Very strong, consistent track record of TOP SALES performance

5) History of stability with no job hopping

6) No major gaps in a resume

7) Challenger with an ability to pleasantly challenge people's mindsets

8) Great image and outgoing personality

9) Great references

10) Do you really like the person? Your customer probably will too.

11) Currently employed

12) Super positive attitude

13) Did the person do his/her homework? Understand what this job will require?

14) Strong work ethic

15) Competitive

These traits should, in total, be the gold standard, but sometimes in your specific open territory or circumstance, the perfect candidate may not exist. The goal is to find someone with as many of the above 15 traits as possible.

1) Burning desire to succeed. Passion.

This may be an area in which lists of questions may help you uncover true desires and feelings. Burning desire is hard to fake, and usually you can flush "fakers" out through several techniques. There are several interviewing styles, and not one of them is wrong. Use whatever technique you find helpful. Some like to use the intimidation method. This method can work for entry-level sales jobs, but for more advanced jobs in which you are trying to hire top people with experience, candidates may view you as difficult and may not want to work for you. That doesn't mean you can't ask tough questions; it's just a matter of how you ask them. It also depends on what kind of company you're working for. If you work for a highly desirable company, you might get away with the intimidator approach. We tend to take a more relaxed interview approach, asking tough questions but in a respectful way.

Keep in mind that people call it recruiting for a reason. You can be the toughest interviewer in the world, but when you find the right person, you had better recruit the person. The great college football coaches recruit great football players. Even though players line up to play for Penn State, when the coach finds the guys he wants, he recruits them. That includes selling them on the school and selling them on coming to play for him. Even when hiring for entry-level positions, even if people really want to work for your company, sell them on the job, on the company, and on working for you.

Again, burning desire, fire in the belly, passion, and enthusiasm are hard to fake. You can not only figure out if a candidate is faking by asking good questions, but also by observing body language and eye contact.

Here are a few questions to use to flush out how driven the candidate really is. Keep in mind that great interviewees can give you all the right answers, but you have to figure out if the person is telling the truth. One way is to ask several similar questions and drill down in the interview.

Anyone can give one great example of success, but a great rep should have multiple examples.

- ◆ Tell me about a time you went above and beyond the call of duty. Many times, candidates can come up with one good answer. Follow up this request with another.

- ◆ Share another example in which you went above and beyond the call of duty. What are your goals?

- ◆ Tell me about your accomplishments in life, starting as far back as you would like to go.

Is there a pattern of success throughout their life? Was he/she a top athlete in high school or college? Was he/she an officer in the high school class, sorority, or fraternity? Has he/she won any awards for top performance in any facet of life? These may not be the deciding factors as to whether you hire someone, but it is a way to see whether the person has possessed a burning desire to be the best throughout their life.

There are many books that have pages and pages of interview questions you might ask. You can find hundreds of great interview questions on line. Pick the most important for your industry. Pick questions with which you feel comfortable and make them a natural part of your conversation.

This mixture of burning desire and passion to be the best is one of the most important qualities to look for. Experience has shown that it is more important than work experience, knowledge, or any other quality. If one possesses this trait, that individual will work incredibly hard to get the experience and knowledge to succeed.

One cautionary note: ensure that the candidate still, in fact, possesses this passion and is not just pulling from past passion, saying the things they used to say when they had the passion. People can be good actors, especially if at one time they possessed the passion. One way to do this is by closely reviewing the person's track record and getting recent references. If the person was "all-world" five years ago but hasn't accomplished much in the last few years, for whatever reason, the person may have lost that enthusiasm. We will discuss this in more detail.

2) Enthusiasm

It has been said that 60% of successful sales is enthusiasm. A candidate can have a burning desire to succeed, but do they have enthusiasm for your industry or products? Why do they want to get into your industry? What excites them about your products? Make sure candidates are interested in your company for the right reasons.

3) Two Years of Sales Experience

This is a requirement unless, of course, you are in a company that hires entry-level salespeople. Every new salesperson has to start somewhere, and there are some great companies that help people get their start. It can be very rewarding to be in a position to teach people the basics of selling.

If you are hiring people without sales experience, ensure the candidate possesses that special brand of passion and burning desire. That's most important. Other requirements may be that they have a decent GPA and a good image.

Hiring someone with sales experience will save you the time of teaching basic selling skills. Depending on your products and industry, your best bet may be to hire the top salesperson who has a few years of experience. Many advanced selling jobs will absolutely require sales experience, so that is what you'll need to hire.

With sales experience, you want it to be TOP SALES, meaning the person's track record must be top notch: Top 10%, Sales Rep of the Year, Rookie of the Year, Award Trips, etc.

4) Very strong, consistent track record of TOP SALES performance

We realize that these sought-after traits are somewhat running together, but they are related and are critical to your success in hiring top salespeople. When you hire someone, you should look for a pattern of success in a sales career and/or in life. If hiring someone with no sales experience, again, look for a track record of success in life. Was he/she a leader in high school? How about leadership positions in college? Did he/she show initiative?

One thing you should understand clearly: Candidates will lie, distort, stretch the truth, and BS you in every way imaginable. This may seem somewhat cynical, but it is a fact of life. Hey, we are the most upbeat positive guys you'll meet, and we DO believe in our fellow man. But to survive in this world, you've got to be real. The reality is that people will say anything to you or put anything on their resume, truthful or not, in order to get a better job. Understanding this fact will help you out tremendously. When interviewing someone, look for reasons **NOT** to hire them, and if they pass that test, they are probably pretty good.

———◆———

Dean:

I was taught this a few years into my management career, and it has served me well. I was taught to look at a resume in a different light. Being basically a positive person, I tended to give people the benefit of the doubt. I wanted to believe they accomplished everything on their resumes. After being burned a couple of times by candidates who lied on their resume, I was told to be more cynical of candidates, disbelieving everything on their resumes until they could prove to me that they actually did the things they said. I became a much better identifier of talent after that lesson.

———◆———

One way to ensure that people have accomplished what they say and that everything on their resume is true, is to take a look at the brag book they brought you. Some managers don't even look at them. Why not? This is a book that has documented proof, letters, pictures of awards, and anything else that can prove they did the things they said they have done. In an entry-level job, ask to see a sealed college transcript, proving the person actually graduated from college. Your company may not require a college degree, which is fine. If your company does require it, and you like the candidate, you had best ask the person to start the process of calling the college registrar because sometimes it will take a few weeks to get it in hand. Go through the brag book with a fine-toothed comb.

———◆———

Dean:

I once interviewed a candidate who had the job hands down. She had been promoted several times within her company, which was well-documented, but the recruiter told her to have a brag book, which she knew I liked to see.

The salesperson panicked because she supposedly did not keep these sorts of documents and letters. She took her boyfriend's performance review, "whited out" his name on the signature page as well as a few other changes and signed her own name. She almost pulled it off, until she got in front of my mentor who caught the fraud. This guy always made it a habit of reading every single word of the final candidate's brag book. This performance review was very lengthy and wordy. It was at least 10 pages long, and most of the grades on the side were of the highest rank. All ones and twos. Next to each category of rank, again, was some very wordy feedback from her manager and somewhere in the middle of the review, almost undetectable to the skimming reader's eyes, were the words, "Bob, great job cold-calling on new customers." Bob? This candidate was a woman named Leslie. My mentor immediately shot down to the signature page and you could clearly see the scattered lines of a poorly done "white-out" job. We shut down the process with this person, and, luckily, I had a strong backup candidate.

This girl could have had the job of her life. Even if she didn't have a strong brag book, we may have hired her anyway. She was very energetic, she had been promoted, and we were trying to hire more women in our sales force. But she chose to lie and got busted. From that point on, I question every detail of a person's resume and what they say. In addition, this experience reinforced another lesson I learned from this mentor:

Always have a backup candidate.

———◆———

You just never know what is going to happen. If you put all your eggs in one basket, you may end up with a lot of egg on your face. What could happen? A candidate may not pass the drug screening test, the current employer may make the person a better offer to stay, he/she may be playing your company with the better offer, he/she may get cold feet about changing jobs, a spouse may talk the person out of it, the candidate may decide to back to school to get an MBA. If you blew off all the other candidates because you thought you had this one in the bag, you may have to start all over again with candidates who may not be anywhere near as strong as your second and third choices, who by now have already accepted jobs from other companies or who simply don't want to be second best.

———◆———

Dean:

I once worked for a very difficult director of sales. I learned a lot about how NOT to lead a team from this guy, but I actually learned a few positive things from him as well. One was to always have a backup candidate. He had all the managers send two candidates to him. During my first go-around with him, he called me after interviewing my two candidates and said, "I think we have a problem with your Number One candidate. Look at the top of his college transcript. You see the word, *ongoing*?" I was dumfounded. It took me weeks to get the transcripts out of this guy, and he bamboozled me. He lied all the way through the process that he had a degree. My mentor felt my other candidate was great and I hired her.

———◆———

Dave:

Another reason for having a backup candidate: I always liked to entertain the prospective candidate and his/her spouse by taking them to dinner. It's amazing what you can learn from a spouse. Many years ago, as I was about to hire a young man, he excused himself to go to the restroom while the three of us were having dinner.. At that very moment, his spouse told me I would be making a huge mistake by hiring her husband. Needless to say, I was dumbfounded. After inquiring as to why, she mentioned that he drank way too much (even though at dinner he did not exhibit this), he had been cheating on her, and she had just filed for divorce two weeks earlier. I know this sounds crazy, but it was all true. We ended the evening without me offering the position to this candidate. He called me the next day expecting an offer, and I informed him I was moving in a different direction. He never asked me why. Thank goodness for the spouse!! The lesson in this is that I always take the spouse/significant other on final interviews. I explain to the spouse that this is a difficult job. The time demands are incredibly tough. The commitment level I expect is high. In other words, I paint a pretty rough picture. I want BOTH of them to know what they are getting themselves into IF my candidate takes this position.

Many of the other attributes that we have mentioned may be obvious: competitive history of success, attitude, etc. One that might be tougher to navigate is attitude. How do you go about discerning someone's attitude? We believe it starts in the first interview. Did he/she prepare for the interview? Did the candidate do his/her homework? Did he/she take the initiative to ride with one of our reps in the field BEFORE the interview to learn more about this opportunity? Some useful questions:

- ♦ Tell me what you know about our business.

- ♦ What are our call points?

- ♦ Tell me about the two most successful products we are currently selling.

- ♦ What do you think our representatives do on a daily basis?

We believe that if someone has not properly prepared for an interview, it shows many things. One, it shows an overall attitude about wanting this position. If someone cannot successfully answer these questions, that person is no longer in consideration. We believe candidates who truly exhibit the traits of desire, hunger, drive, superb attitude, and competitive spirit will be able to easily answer those simple questions about your product and your company.

5) History of stability with no job hopping.

What's a job hopper? Anyone with four or more jobs in 10 years is a job hopper. Anyone with three jobs in five years is a job hopper. The reality is if a person has a pattern of bouncing every 1.5 – 3 years, there is a very good chance the person will leave your company in 1.5 – 3 years.

6) No major gaps in a resume.

The first sign someone has a gap or gaps in their resume is the use of whole number years instead of breaking out the months. For instance, they put down 2001 – 2004 versus June 2001 – September 2004. Sometimes things happen in life. If you work long enough, you will have a gap in your resume; company lay-offs; failed clinical trials; company fails; etc. It's not a deal killer, but lying about a gap or trying to hide it may call a candidate into question. There are unreasonable managers out there. If someone had 10 years of an award-winning track record and found himself in a tough situation but he is able to tell you in a positive way about the situation, you might continue interviewing him rather than give up on that person. Sometimes circumstances are impossible for even the strongest of people. Of course, you wonder why someone left a job without finding another first, but it could be that the situation was impossible or unavoidable.

The main thing to look for is whether the person has a logical, reasonable reason for the gap. If he says he just wanted to travel around Europe for six months that might not be a great answer. He might be hiding something. "I just decided I needed a change" might also mean he is hiding something.

7) Challenger . . .

. . . with an ability to pleasantly challenge people's mindsets

Again, please read the book, *THE CHALLENGER SALE*. In today's complex sales environment, sales people must bring real value to the table and must be willing to challenge the mindset of their customers. Be sure to ask questions surrounding the candidate's ability to use this selling technique.

8) Great image and outgoing personality

Self-explanatory. We've all inherited sales people that really bothered customers or bothered you and the other team members. How does this happen? How did they get hired? Don't let it happen on your watch.

9) Great references

You must check references yourself. Many companies tell their managers not to give references, but you can bet that if someone calls another manager about someone who was one of their best former sales reps, you have to worry. If you call former managers and they go on and on about how great your candidate is and advise you to hire them as fast as you can, that's a pretty good sign. If they basically just confirm they worked there and half-heartedly say, "Oh, Bob, he was good," that's not quite the resounding endorsement you should be looking for. How about something more like, "Man, Bob, you've got to hire that guy. He was by far my best rep during the time I was his manager. This guy will run through walls for you. I'd hire him back in a second. Don't lose that guy. He's an A+ selling machine."

Don't talk yourself into someone because you just want to get the process over. If someone was incredible, usually their former mentors will tell you that without a worry of being sued; but if they weren't that great, they may not return your calls.

10) Do you really like the person? Your customers probably will, too.

Don't hire someone solely because of a track record or because someone else thinks you should hire that person. You have to work with the rep. It is like a marriage. Do you like this person? Is your gut saying, "This is the one."? They don't have to be your favorite person in the world, but their personality should be pleasant.

11) Currently Employed?

This shouldn't be a deal killer, but it should raise questions. You just need to uncover the logic and reason behind unemployment. Again, you work long enough, and you'll encounter downsizings, shutdowns, and other career challenges. You just need to get a good understanding as to why someone is unemployed. Was it a good decision? Does it make sense?

12) Super positive attitude

Many studies show that the top salespeople have incredible optimism. In fact, in the book *LEARNED OPTIMISM*, Martin Seligman discovered through various studies that optimism is the Number One trait of top salespeople. *SUCCESS THROUGH A POSITIVE MENTAL ATTITUDE* by Napoleon Hill is a great book. Negativity is the road block to all success.

13) Did the person do his/her homework?

Does the person understand what this job will require? Did the candidate learn about your products? Did he/she know your call points?

14) Strong work ethic

You can uncover this through a good line of questions. What did the person do out of the ordinary to go beyond the call of duty for customers? How many hours does a person work a week? Look at the candidate's entire life. Did the person put himself/herself through college? If not, did the person still work during college?

15) **Competitive**

Again, see what the candidate has done throughout his entire life. What accomplishments has he achieved? Was he/she an athlete? Has he/ she won awards in the past? Ask if rankings and awards are important.

---◆---

Dean:

As I look back over all my interviewing and hiring, the great candidates I hired were pretty obvious early in the process. Consider all the methods of interviewing, such as interviewing 40 candidates before you even consider hiring someone. Review all the interview tactics people employ, such as being a mean, tough intimidator versus coming off relaxed and conversational in order to get people to relax and open up. Think about the thousands of questions that can be asked. The reality is that no matter what approach you take, if you look for someone with the above traits (don't expect all of them), you will make some great hires. It's when you struggle to find a reason to hire someone or when you try to lead a person to tell you what you want to hear, you have probably found an average candidate at best.

---◆---

Dave:

Bottom line, after continued interviewing of your top candidates, the cream will rise to the top. You should always feel better about the second interview than the first with your top candidate. The same holds true for the third, fourth, and fifth interviews. Always feel better each time you see the person.

10

HOW TO TEAR APART A RESUME

The closest most people come to perfection is when they fill out a job application.

- Don L. Griffith

. . . or they write their resume!

FIRST THING TO LOOK FOR on a resume is if only years are used on a timeline. Have the candidate tell you when he/she started a job and when he stopped. Uncover any gaps. When someone uses just years, the candidate is usually hiding gaps. Gaps aren't deal breakers, especially as someone gets more tenured. If you are 32 years old, are a new manager, and don't have a gap on your resume, don't get too cocky and arrogant. By the time you retire at 65, you, too, will probably have a gap on your resume.

Find out why each job change was made. Make sure there is a good reason that makes logical sense. If there is a gap, make sure to verify the reason. It's somewhat humorous that if you use a good line of questioning (and it's not that hard if you listen), you can spot a lie a mile away. People start to squirm, their answers don't flow anymore, and they don't make sense.

Gaps aren't a problem necessarily, but if there is a gap between every job, you may have someone who:

1) doesn't make great decisions
2) quits too easily
3) may have performance issues
4) gets bored easily
5) is willing to take a lot of risk
6) is a hired gun mercenary

Sometimes people just have a bad run with two jobs. An example: An unpredicted layoff occurs, and a consulting company just comes in and chops headcounts without regard to success or other factors. It does happen. You'll just have to explore a little more. Maybe they had to get a job fast and unfortunately bad fortune strikes again. Did this happen? Or did they just take the second job in order to buy time for a better job? What was their track record prior to the double bounce? Five plus years at another company with a stellar track record?

We've all worked for horrible mentors or been in very tough situations. Is your candidate the first to jump ship? Or are they the last to get in the life boat? If they are the first, they may be the first to jump ship when your company hits some rough waters, and every company does. You want people who will weather the storm.

Then there are those who get bored every two years. They just do. If you ask good questions, you can usually decipher the type by their answers. If you have a tough territory to fill and you find a candidate who seems to knock down a lot of business in a short amount of time, but they've bounced, you might have another colleague interview them to see if they pick up on some squirrely answers. There's nothing wrong with getting other opinions on your top candidates. People with different interviewing styles might pick up on things you missed.

In start-up situations, you may need to hire some people with relationships to get the ball rolling. There are those people who just go from start up to start up.

That's what they do, and they love it. That doesn't mean there is anything wrong with it if you are involved with a startup as well but in general you don't want to hire job hoppers. If you are in a mature company with a mature product line, they're not the right candidates for you. Need some sales and some sales fast, tenured people, who are STILL GREAT sales reps with solid relationships might be the way you have to go, and that's ok.

Look for fluff. If someone says they were Number One out of 16 in the second and third quarters, what is more important is how the person finished for the year.

Finishing No. 15 out of 16 overall will negate any impressive second- and third-quarter standings.

If a candidate says he/she finished 110% of plan or quota in 2006, ask quickly, before the person has time to think, how the entire company finished against quota in 2006. If the company finished at 115%, that means that the average rep was 115% of plan and the candidate was at 110%. That's below average.

If someone says he/she was 120% of plan in Q1 and 105% in Q2, and 112% in Q3, but leave off Q4, ask them what their % of plan was in Q4 and overall for the year. You may find he was 69% in Q4 and finished 101% of plan. That may be good, that may be OK, or that may be bad. How did the rest of the company do?

Have him expand on his accomplishments: "No. 2 in the region." How many reps are in the region? Two? Four? No. 2 in what? Maybe he/she was No. 2 in gross sales. Maybe he/she was No. 2 in % increase. If that's the case, what were sales the year before? Maybe the territory only had $5,000 in sales and now it has $10,000 in sales. Maybe the No. 3 rep had $250,000 in sales and grew it to $350,000. Even though Rep No. 1 grew his/her business 100% and Rep No. 2 grew business by 40%, who had the more impressive accomplishment? It's better to find out what the overall ranking was.

Some reps will say they were No. 1 in the country with a specific product, but it may have been with a low cost unimportant product. It looks good on paper, that Number One flashing in your face. A manager who doesn't understand that particular business might think that is impressive. Others who do understand that business realize that being No. 1 in that unimportant product line isn't impressive. For instance, in interventional procedures performed in the cath lab of a hospital, diagnostic wires are somewhat of a commodity product that salespeople don't normally focus on. You might ask the candidate, "Are diagnostic wires a focus product for your company? What were the total sales of that product in your territory? What were the total sales of your top selling product? How much do diagnostic wires cost? How much do your most expensive products cost?" Most companies selling diagnostic wires also sell stents and balloons. Diagnostic wires cost $10. Stents cost $1,500. Balloons cost $200. These questions allow you to drill down into the claims people make.

How did the reps rank overall with all products? If a candidate tells you his/her company didn't produce rankings, look at the company. Medtronic, J&J, Baxter, Boston Scientific—medium to large companies almost always print monthly rankings. Even smaller companies usually rank people. Only occasionally do companies not rank their people.

Note: If all a company sells are commodity products, don't fool yourself into thinking that the candidate doesn't know how to sell. Maybe all a company makes are diagnostic wires, but if a salesperson is in the top 10% of a company like that, he/ she is probably a great salesperson. Have you ever sold a commodity without just selling on price? If a sales rep can sell a commodity based on its features and benefits, he/she may rule the world when selling more technical or advanced products. Again, great sales people are usually driven and excellent no matter what they sell, but they've got to have the passion to sell your products.

---◆---

Dean:

The first medical company I worked for sold products that were considered commodities by material managers, but there were actual differences in the products that end users could appreciate if you were good enough to explain them or sell them. Those who did well selling surgical gloves, surgical drapes, and wound care products, were incredible salespeople. If you can get a surgeon to yell and scream about their surgical drapes, you're a pretty good rep.

Our entire group of surgical sales reps and managers were moved to another division within the company. The director of sales at the new division had a somewhat pompous attitude and stated that the entire team of salespeople and managers was worthless because we sold these supposed "commodity" products. Eventually, 90% of the sales force had enough of this guy and left. I maneuvered my way into what was the most sought-after division of the company, which sold even more technical and expensive products than the second division. I brought over three of the TOP reps who worked for me at the "commodity company." All three of them shot up to the top of the rankings of this technically advanced (non- commodity) company. Now, I didn't actually start this trend, but I helped kick start it. A few years earlier, a guy by the name of Doug Elkin was brought over and became an immediate success. I was brought over and did very well. I recognized that I had some tremendous people who worked for me back at the old company, and I brought the cream of the crop with me. Soon a few of us helped bring over the big Kahuna, Dave Goldin, and he raised the bar again on all of us, breaking all sorts of management records.

It's interesting to see how trends start. Some of the managers started to believe, since a few reps from our old company became all-stars, that if you worked for this "commodity division," you must be great. A few managers made the mistake of hiring average and below-average people from this same company, and they failed. The message is that great salespeople, no matter what they sell, will USUALLY be great anywhere they go, but average reps, no matter what they sell, will usually remain average no matter where they go. The only limiting factor will be the mental ability or intelligence to grasp the new, more technical products. All three people who came to that company with me were bright individuals. In the end, probably 20 people were brought over from this commodity division, and 80% of them did extremely well. Many advanced into management and higher levels of leadership.

So, the second message is to be very careful making judgments or assumptions about what people sell. Great salespeople, and great leaders are great—period.

<hr>

Many people will claim they were or are in the Top 10% of the sales force. When they say this without breaking out the exact ranking, there is a high probability they are just making it up. Quickly ask them, "How many reps were in the company? What was your exact rank?" Do they stumble? Do they say they don't know exactly? "Well, if there were 90 reps, were you No. 9 or No. 2?" You have to decide if you believe them. "How do you know you were Top 10%?" Often, they'll respond, "I just knew based on feedback I was given." Someone might say in order to substantiate his claim of being in the Top 10%, "I was on track to win the award trip." Well, did you win the award trip? Isn't it much more believable when they say, "I was ranked No. 3 of 39 reps" quickly and without hesitation?

But better than just a smooth interviewee is someone who can back it up with proof. The big question is at the end. Does he/she have a brag book to substantiate all the claims made on the resume? He says he was No. 3 of 39 reps. Do you have a ranking report to prove it? Did you win a trip? Did you receive an e-mail or a letter congratulating you? Did you win a plaque? Will a former manager(s) verify he/she won these awards? So many reps will say,

"I never thought it was important or would be important in the future, so I didn't keep that stuff." This is a red flag.

Someone says, "Trained new sales reps" on his/her resume. Was he/she an official field sales trainer? Many times, a candidate will say, "Uh, no, I didn't have an official title as trainer, but I trained people." Were there official trainers in your company? If yes, why didn't the company make you an official trainer?

No date next to education may mean the candidate never received a degree. It may also mean he feels he is too old and thus is hiding a graduation date. As strange as most people or candidates may feel your question is, ask "Did you receive your degree?"

Salesperson of the Year for four consecutive years from 2003-2006 in an organization of 10 salespeople or more is a highly improbable occurrence. A small company may not award a salesperson of the year, but yet some candidates will, in effect, award themselves this title. They rationalize that had the company had this award, he/she should have received it. Remember, people will say anything on a resume. It is your job to decipher what is the truth. A candidate may work in a company of three salespeople, and the other two may be inside customer service people. People often make these sorts of claims when they weren't really in a real sales capacity but heard that these are the things managers look for on resumes.

What was your grade point average? "About 3.0" Was it 3.0; 3.1, or 2.9? Most people know their GPA to the point. "About" is unacceptable. Let the candidate know that you will need their sealed college transcript, so if it was 2.9, that's OK, but you need to know if it was 3.0 or less. Many people will say about 3.0, and then when you get their transcripts it is 2.6. You may have decided to hire that person at 2.6, but now that the person has lied to you, pass on that individual.

By now, you get the picture. Question every detail and you will hire better people. Make sure you are getting the person you thought you were getting.

11

DON'T MISS OUT DUE TO TUNNEL VISION

NOW THAT WE HAVE GIVEN you some insight into how to increase the odds of finding great candidates, be smart enough to know when a true winner walks through the door but doesn't fit the mold you've created. Don't get such a bad case of tunnel vision that the next home run king is sitting in front of you, and you can't see it.

Remember: heart, passion, and drive are what really separates great salespeople from the average. While you can minimize your mistakes in hiring by making sure a candidate isn't a job hopper, has a verifiable track record of success, and has impeccable references, every once in a while, you'll find someone who screams winner without meeting the criteria we've discussed. You've got to be very, very careful. Remember, who you hire can make or break you. Gambling is not the way to win in this game. But sometimes, in your heart, you know everything about a person says "winner." "champion," "award winner." You may not want to take a gamble early in your management career, but as you get experience under your belt, talent scouts of greatness know how to spot winners.

Maybe an individual has one too many jobs, maybe his/her previous industry just doesn't provide rankings (such as the mortgage or real estate industry), or maybe instead of two years of sales experience, he/she only has 1.5 years. But as you talk to him/her, you feel a sense of urgency. You hear the intense and burning desire. You look inside and see of passion flowing throw the person's body.

Great hiring managers have used this term throughout the ages. What is this "it"? They try to describe "it" to others or to HR directors. It's one of the things you have to possess; it's one of the things you have to see and feel. It is difficult to describe what "it" is unless you possess "it." "It" is being on fire with passion and enthusiasm. "It" is very, very difficult to fake, but the reason you must be careful when using this wild card is that some people out there can fake "it." So, until you get really good at spotting those with "it," go with the high odds success factors we've described.

———◆———

Dean:

Sometimes we learn from great teachers, and we take their sage advice as absolute. In everything in life, keep an open mind. The reality is that in sales, probably 70% of the salespeople are average or below average, regardless of the industry they are in. Those who are great usually can be great in any industry. Yes, there are exceptions. Yes, sometimes a great rep selling capital equipment can't sell disposables, but usually that's not the case. Sometimes we get so stuck on certain hot buttons it causes us to pass over some great candidates. Because I was taught to have a certain bias against reps with a certain type of industry background, for my entire career I never interviewed or hired people with that sort of background. I've now seen managers find great salespeople who came from this industry. Most of the time, finding a great salesperson comes back to the human being, not the industry he/she comes from. What's in the heart—that's what matters the most. When your job requires experience in a certain industry, by all means hire the experience, but when faced with a tough geography or the ability to hire from many backgrounds, keep an open mind.

Questions we ask in interviews can also become absolutes in your mind. Questions are great filters when used in their entirety, but be careful. Just because someone answers one question wrong, and it happens to be your "favorite" question, don't pass on a great candidate. That candidate may be nervous; he/she may not understand the question. You may wrongly disqualify a potentially tremendous hire. Many managers pass on phenomenal candidates who go on to get other jobs and do very well.

12

SUMMARY FOR HIRING GREAT PEOPLE

1) DON'T LET ANYONE PUSH YOU into hiring someone you don't feel is the best candidate—not your VP/director of sales, region director, or one of your customers. You are the one who must live with that person and that decision for possibly a long time. Your mentor may keep you from raising the performance of your team. You'll have customers who may come to you and ask you to hire a friend, relative, or the daughter of a friend. Don't do it unless that person is the best candidate for the job.

2) Listen to your inner voice or gut. Usually it is right. You may have been interviewing for a long time and are tired of the process. Your territory may have been open for a long time, and you really feel you need to hire someone. You've found a decent candidate on paper and verbally the person seems pretty good. However, something tells you there is something missing or there is something wrong with this candidate. You may sense he/she will be difficult to manage. Things aren't adding up. Unless you can get some really strong recommendations from former managers, don't make the offer.

3) If someone seems like a great person, but everything is telling you he/she is just average, all the coaching and motivation on your part will probably NOT make that person above average. Plus, even if you could somehow transform an individual, it is going to take a lot of energy on your part. Just go with a candidate who is already a "winner."

4) You must conduct thorough background checks. If references aren't jumping up and down telling you to hire this person, you might want to go on to the next candidate. Many companies tell their managers never to provide detailed references to anyone. If someone asks if an individual

worked at the company, you are usually instructed to just confirm employment. The reason is usually for protection against lawsuits. If you say something bad about someone, that person can sue your company.

However, if candidates are as good as they say they are, having won awards, cooperated, were team players, etc., former managers will usually break the rules and tell you that you should hire them as fast as you can. References may rave for 15 minutes as to how great a person was when working for them.

The managers of representatives who were average or below usually just confirm they worked for the company. This is a red flag. Don't buy into a manager refusing to tell you anything about someone because it's against the company rules. It's usually a sign the person was: 1) average, 2) below average, or 3) difficult to manage. What people don't say is often as informative as what they do say.

---◆---

Dean:

I've hired 44 people during my 15 years of management. Most were excellent hires, but five were bad. I can honestly say that with all five bad hires my gut was telling me not to hire them, but my emotions got the best of me. Luckily, these five hires were spread out over my career, allowing me to build six award-winning teams despite the few bad choices.

Bad hire No. 1 – Great guy, but no fire in the belly. Had a track record on paper, but I failed to get great references. He was moving from a capital equipment sales field outside the operating room to implant sales opportunities in the OR. A lot of time had passed, and I couldn't fill this difficult territory. I liked him as a person and gave him a chance. I thought he would be coachable and driven, but he failed on both counts.

Bad hire No. 2 – Once again, tough territory to fill. This rep was a master schmoozer and big talker. He talked a big game and indicated he knew everyone west of the Rockies. Big name dropper. All sorts of success, so he claimed. Again, I broke my cardinal rule and failed to get great background references. He ended up being lazy and only had a few relationships.

Bad hire No. 3 – She could have done the job and done it well, but she wanted the job for all the wrong reasons. She was trying to relocate to Phoenix for a fiancé. Never hire someone who wants to get to a city for the wrong reasons. While it is illegal to bring this stuff up in an interview, if the person brings it up, know that nine out of 10 times, moves for boyfriends, girlfriends, and fiancés almost NEVER work out. I've hired two great people for relocations, but they were for the right reasons. In this case, once the engagement broke off, she disengaged from the job, fell apart, and never lived up to her potential.

Bad hire No. 4 – I hired a distributor who promised $1 million worth of business. It all sounded good until a competitor for whom he used to sell threatened him and my company with a lawsuit. My company decided not to risk it and didn't move forward with the contract with this distributor. We tried to patch it together with another rep who had worked with him. He was going to help her for a year, behind the scenes, until his non-compete ran out. They began to fight, and it became a time-consuming nightmare that never produced anything. He never helped her, and we never got the $1 million in business. Longer term, the woman we hired to work with him ended up doing well, but in the short term it was a mistake.

Lessons:
♦ Talk is cheap
♦ Unless you are a startup, in orthopedics or wine sales, avoid distributors. Always go with a direct sales force when you can.

Bad hire No. 5 – This was tough territory to fill and we had a terrible time crunch. He was hired by committee and all of us gave thumbs up, but in the end, the buck stops at my desk. I must take responsibility for the ultimate hire. He promised the world. Got surgeons to call on his behalf, but they never produced for him. He never worked, and we suspected he was doing side deals.

I was fortunate to have hired a lot of outstanding salespeople, many of whom went on to become award-winning sales reps, managers, and VPs themselves. I used the techniques we have described in order to insure successful hires.

Dave:

Hiring Top Talent is the Most Important Job You Have as a Manager!
When you hire the best, your job as a leader becomes so much easier. You've empowered your team to make decisions. The team trusts and believes in you because you trust and believe in them. Challenge your new hires. Set the expectations high. Inspect what you expect. What do I mean? If you have set the expectation with your new representative to finish first in the training class, follow up daily with the trainers. Ask how your new person is doing. Fly into the city where the training is being held and show your new hire that you care. I can tell you, average managers never do this. If your new superstar sees you sitting in the back of the class offering encouragement and support, WOW! Most likely, you've got a new representative who will run through walls for you!

13

BE A STUDENT OF THE GAME

Education will not simply be a prelude to a career, but a lifelong endeavor.

- Maud Barkley

LIKE ANYTHING YOU WANT TO be good at in life, you must continue learning. You must "keep your ax sharp." If being a manager is what you want to be, and this is what will put money in your pocket, you must continually strive to be better, not only as a manager but also as a human being. Doctors and lawyers are continually reading journals, papers, and updates on their profession. Why wouldn't you make the same effort to ensure you are the best at what you do? Make it a point to devote 15 minutes a day to reading something that will make you a better manager. Granted, you are reading this book; however, it may have been required reading.

In addition, make it a point to have weekly conversations with other successful managers, both inside and outside your company. Go to leadership conferences. Surely your company will pick up the tab.

Be an active participant when your company provides management and leadership training. Often, people feel they have their jobs "down." They feel training is a waste of time. They are physically in the meetings but mentally they are "checked out." As long as you must be there, why not try to learn something? It might not even be a matter of learning something new, but, rather, it might be an opportunity to remind yourself about the things that once made you successful that you have quit doing.

Being a student of the game also means staying on top of your products as well as technical and clinical information. You will need to bring value to discussions with customers, and if they figure out you don't know what you are talking about, you will embarrass your sales rep and yourself.

Dean:

Don't try to reinvent the wheel. Find great managers and discern what they're doing to be successful. Most great salespeople and managers got there because not only are they good at what they do, but they also like to help people. I was lucky to have learned from my dad, Gerry, Dave, Rick, Jim, Debbie, Charlie, Jeff, Chris, Manny, Chris, Scott, Ryan, Bob, Matt, Neal and David. Don't be afraid to let them know how much you appreciate their help and guidance.

Also understand and realize that there will be salespeople whom you will mentor. You will become very close friends, and they will keep in touch with you for the rest of your life. They will thank you and appreciate the opportunities you give them and the knowledge you impart to them. It will be very rewarding. On the other side of the coin, you will give people tremendous opportunities. You will support them in "rack and stack" meetings and help them get promoted. Sadly, through it all, they will never thank you, they'll never stay in touch, and in their mind and publicly, they will feel they did it all on their own. Understand that both types of people are just a normal piece of humanity. Be happy for both types, and don't let the latter get you down. It's just the way it is.

Dave:

Take the initiative to learn. Learning isn't easy unless you want to be better. Ask a lot of questions. Find a mentor. Ask that mentor to advise and counsel you. Learn from the best. My mentor early on was a gentleman with whom I had nothing in common, other than the fact he was a winner, and I wanted to be the winner he was. I wanted to follow him because he was a winner and a leader in our business. He knew everybody. He had a following because he knew how to build a team. His team ALWAYS wanted to be around him. Why? The main reason was that he was always teaching. He was an incredible coach! He was fun to be around.

Unfortunately, the wrong priorities took over his life. Because of some poor personal choices he made, he lost some luster, respect, and leadership. However, in his prime, he was the best!

14

EVALUATE THE TALENT YOU HAVE INHERITED

Business is like roller skating; either you keep moving or you fall down.

- Doc Blakely, humorist

SO IS MANAGEMENT. YOU'VE GOT to keep setting new goals, raising the bar, evaluating your talent, coaching people to higher achievements, and keeping things fresh.

As you become a new manager and have filled your open territories, you must then begin the process of evaluating your current sales representatives. Not only must you begin evaluating them, but you must also begin the process of coaching and developing them to become the best they can be. Where do you begin? The first thing you should do is get out of your office and into the field with your sales representatives. Unfortunately, for many average managers, evaluating, coaching, and developing salespeople are not core priorities. When companies force them to do it, it pains them. They look at it as administrative work that wastes time, but this is the furthest thing from the truth. You owe it to your people to let them know where they stand. It opens up dialogue that can make people better.

◆

Dean:

You certainly want to get the support and backing of your sales leaders. Right out of the gate, you should be communicating with them. When you first interviewed for your management job, you may have competed with some of the reps you will inherit. They may be feeling rejected and overlooked—sometimes downright mad. You need to get out with them, get them back on track as strong leaders on the team. Assure them that you will support them and help them reach the next step of their careers. After I am able to get my leaders on board, I usually focus on my weakest link and begin assessing what needs to be done to move that person up or, unfortunately, sometimes out. I always take a supportive posture in dealing with the weak link initially. I like to give people the benefit of the doubt, but I also expect action.

I always get a kick out of the fact that one of my "bad" hires made this comment to me as I prepared to visit him. "Why do you come ride with me all the time? No one ever did that at XYZ. I've never had a manager ride with me."

My response to him was, "First, I only ride with you about once every two months. If I didn't ride with you and all the other sales reps, what do you think the company would be paying me to do? Sit in my office in my boxer shorts and drink coffee all day?

Secondly, they may not have done this at XYZ, which I find hard to believe, but I'm going to be riding with you at least once every two months. I have seven reps, and with a possible week for a meeting, I'll be back here again. My guess is that if your former manager didn't ride with you, he was spending his time in the office, and he wasn't a very good manager."

———◆———

Dave:

I believe that getting into the field and assessing your talent are paramount tasks. However, I always start with my superstar or the person I perceive to be the leader of the peer group within my team. Experience has taught me that if I can win over the leader, the leader will help "sell" the other team members that my style, desire to make them better individuals, and ability to support them when needed, are valuable traits. I want that leader to believe in me! If I can convince him/her of my abilities, it paves the way for others on the team to really listen when I am coaching.

There is certainly a balance that you need to strike. If you are just becoming a manager and start being heavy-handed right out of the gate, you will cause immediate dissention on your team. For the first few months, you will want to be an observer. Your presence in the field will send a message to the team that you are going to be an "active" manager and not hide in your office. You are going to work to understand their territories, their customers, their challenges, and them.

As you are evaluating your team, you want to build trust and support so that you won't have a mutiny on your hands when tough decisions or changes need to be made. Understand that salespeople often stick together like a pack of wolves. If you immediately go into a division or region and begin firing or putting people on performance plans, the entire team will feel threatened and may believe you are out to get them all, personally and individually. Whether justified or not, you may find yourself answering questions from HR. If, however, you build confidence and trust that you are working in the best interest of the individual and the team, when you have to make some "moves" on people, the rest will understand and will not try to undermine your efforts.

So, what do you want to look for during your field visits?

1) Do reps know their products? If they don't, you may need to get them help. You may also need to determine why they don't know their products. How did they do in sales training? How long has it been since sales training? Is it a matter of their not getting proper training, or is it a lack of effort on their part? If it is a matter of not getting the proper training from the sales training department, then you need to get them up to speed. This can be accomplished through the sales training department, through their field sales trainer, or through a fellowship with a customer. If it is an issue of not putting forth the effort, then you need to have a discussion with the rep and get that person up to speed.

2) Do they know their customers? If not, this can be a red flag that they are not working very hard or don't know how to get in to see customers. You need to observe what they are doing on a daily basis and determine which of the two it is. If a sales rep isn't working hard, the person will understand that you are on to him/her. Often, slacking salespeople will either "kick it in gear" or will leave the company. One way to get a good idea if someone is working is to do a three-day field visit. Anyone can put together a day, maybe two days of customer visits. The rep simply calls the best customers and brings you to see them. Trying to put together three consecutive days of solid appointments may be hard for those not working hard.

If a sales rep does not understand how to get in to see the customers, then you need to show him/her or get a field sales trainer to go back through the process. You may need to have the sales rep spend another day or two with a top representative to learn effective methods.

3) How are their selling skills? Do they understand the sales process? If reps are having a problem with the sales process, you may need to coach them. You might also enroll them in a basic or advanced selling course.

4) How are their customer relationships? Do their customers seem to like them? If not, a basic selling course MAY help them improve this area. Some salespeople are not very likeable. You may have a problem that you will eventually need to address. You may need to get rid of a particular person if there is a major problem with the way customers relate to the person. Is he/she open to coaching? This is a tough one. If someone's personality is irritating, it may be quite a project to change one's personality. This may be a situation in which a third party might be necessary. How do you tell someone that people don't like him/her? From an HR standpoint, you must be careful. This is subjective criticism. You will need to document examples in which customers are not responding in order to validate your points.

5) Are they pulling products out of the bag? Are they merely talking about products or are they demonstrating products? Are they asking good, open-ended questions? Are they using documented clinical/technical papers, brochures, and demos, or are they just talking off the cuff? Are they even talking about products or just doing PR work, shaking hands, and bringing in doughnuts? Are they challenging customers and their way of thinking? Even long-term, tenured reps get to the point in which they rely on relationships, almost solely, rather than relying on their selling abilities. Often it is the tenured salespeople who complain when the company has everyone attend a basic selling course when, in fact, they can benefit from the course as much as a rookie. As managers and as salespeople, we must always go back to the basics and ensure we are doing the

things that will make us successful.

6) Are they reading customers properly? Sometimes reps don't see the "buying" signals. Sometimes salespeople don't notice that they are going down the wrong path with customers. Sometimes they don't realize it is a bad time for the customers or that they are irritating clients. In short, they don't "read' the customer. You, as an outside observer, can help.

7) Do they ask for the business? This is one of the biggest mistakes for many salespeople—and managers, for that matter. They take the customer through the sales process beautifully but fail to execute the final, most important step of all: They fail to CLOSE! They interview the customer beautifully. They ask open-ended questions. They find out the customer's needs. They demonstrate the products better than anyone. They find out the customer's concerns. They negotiate. Then, in the end, they're afraid or forget to ask for the order.

8) Are they organized? Do they keep their detail bag organized? Do they bring a detail bag on all calls? Are their demonstration kits well thought out and organized? Do they utilize the tools the company provides to help them sell products? Are they using the selling brochures to discuss the products in an organized manner and then asking for the business? Are they coming up with new approaches to sell your products and sharing their successes with others?

As you observe behavior in the field, you can provide valuable feedback for improvement. How do you provide this feedback? 1) You must do it verbally, and 2) You must follow it up with a Field Visit Letter. You, as manager, must make the determination as to whether each representative is worth keeping on your team.

15

THE DREADED FIELD VISIT LETTER (FVL)

Successful people form the habit of doing what failures don't like to do. They like the results they get by doing what they don't necessarily enjoy.

- Earl Nightingale

NO ONE PARTICULARLY LIKES FIELD visit letters. Most sales representatives hate them because 70-80% of reps are average or below average and know that the letter will potentially shine a negative light on his/her performance during the week. The salespeople aren't stupid, and while they realize their manager is trying to coach them and give feedback, they also know that the letters can be used against them.

Many managers don't like FVLs because

- ◆ they are extra administrative work.
- ◆ they know that some resistance or defensiveness from their sales team may result.

YOU MUST DO FIELD VISIT LETTERS for several reasons:

1) **You owe it to your salespeople to give them feedback** on how you feel they are performing throughout the year. You can't just do a year-end review and out of the blue, suddenly spring three things on them at the end of the year that concern you. This will really cause friction and defensiveness. And what is the first thing they are going to say to HR or to you? "Why didn't you tell me you had a problem with that?" Bottom line, there should be no surprises because during the field travel you have openly communicated both the good things AND the improvements needed.

2) **You owe it to your salespeople to actually help them**. You are a trained observer. You will see and catch things that salespeople may not even know they are doing. Michael Jordan always had a coach. No coach would claim to be a better player than Michael, yet you can be assured that if he was slipping into a slump or mechanically doing something wrong, he wanted his coaches to point it out and get him back on track. Shaquille O'Neal will be considered one of the great centers of all time, but don't you think he wanted help with his free throws? And when he was coached, he got better at free throws.

3) **You need to document everything with your salespeople**. Listen, you will develop some great relationships and friendships with some of your salespeople that will last the rest of your life. But, while your salespeople are working for you, you are still the mentor, and you need to be the mentor. You will still have to take action if someone is not performing. You have to avoid allowing friendships to get in the way of doing your job. When salespeople are backed into a corner, unfortunately, in today's litigious society, they will often do what they have to do to protect themselves and their jobs, even if that means lying.

As long as you document everything, you will be protected. Create a paper trail, and when you consistently do field visit letters with your reps, they know you have the documentation. They know that they need to keep their performance at a peak and that they can't try to claim any falsehoods against you. Field visit letters are the greatest coaching, developing, and liability protection tool you have at your disposal. Each should only take 10 minutes, so just do them.

16

THE PURPOSE OF THE FIELD VISIT AND THE LETTER

If your actions inspire others to dream more, learn more, do more and become more, you are a leader.
- John Quincy Adams, sixth president of the United States

WHAT ARE YOUR GOALS FOR the field visit? Again, it's important for you and the sales reps to understand why you do the FVL and what's in it for them.

- ♦ **Rep development** – This is the most powerful tool you have to provide rep development. If you consistently follow up each field visit with a verbal discussion, then a written summary of that discussion, you can create an atmosphere of communication and provide crucial development. Haphazardly throw out criticism or surprise feedback, and the rep could take it as threatening and uncaring.

- ♦ **Build relationships with key customers** – By letting your sales team know that during your visits you would like to visit some of the key customers, they will come to understand that you are not just coming out to waste their time or to merely watch their every move. Many times, 50% or more of your income is derived by how well your sales teams do. The customers are not just their customers, but they are your customers and the company's customers. You owe it to the sales rep, yourself, and the company to get out and visit with these people. The FVL gives you an opportunity to openly discuss how you will both manage these important customers.

- ♦ **Rep morale: Put yourself in the representative's position** – One of the most de-motivating and frustrating things for salespeople is to go six months or a year thinking that they are doing a great job, especially because they received no feedback from their superior to the contrary, then be told that they are failing. What often happens is one month after the year is over and it's time for bonuses, merit increases, or pay raises, the managers are forced to do year-end performance reviews. Some managers, if it wasn't demanded, wouldn't even do a year-end review. So out of nowhere the manager unloads on salespeople in a documented performance review. He/she lets the weakest people know that they aren't doing the job. It can cause a lot of unnecessary anger and mistrust. How do you avoid this surprise while building trust and loyalty? Give consistent feedback through the year through FVLs. If you do that, the final performance review for the year won't be a surprise and your poor performers will know their bad review is coming and that potentially a warning letter or performance plan may soon follow.

In addition to constructive coaching, remember that many salespeople crave recognition and a pat on the back. In a FVL, you should focus on one or two major things that need work that will have a positive impact on sales commission and, thus, their commission dollars. The FVL is an excellent opportunity to also focus on the great things they are doing and a great time to give that deserved pat on the back. At the same time, you are also giving constructive coaching on no more than two areas where improvement is needed.

Many managers make the mistake of only communicating with their people when something is wrong. If you want to really drive the morale and sales numbers on your team, try finding things they do well at least twice as often as the things they aren't doing so well. Yes, part of being a great manager is about motivating and being somewhat of a cheerleader. If you only got into management for the power and the opportunity to browbeat others, then you chose the wrong profession.

♦ **Performance and other company issues** – As we discussed earlier, the FVL is an important legal document as well. Unfortunately, if a salesperson is not getting the job done, the "not so fun part" of being a manager is having to get rid of people. It's one of the job requirements, and if you can't stomach or do this part of the job… also the wrong profession.

What you must always remind yourself is that you owe it to the company to sometimes take action on someone. You also owe it to that person, and you owe it to yourself and your family. If you provide your salespeople with the education, the feedback, and the opportunity to succeed, and they fail to work hard and to really try to succeed, then you must take action. It is not your fault that they couldn't make it. If in your heart you know you have to let people go due to job performance, and it IS your fault because you didn't do the proper job in developing them and ensuring they were properly trained, then again, it might be time for you to choose another profession. As a manager, you also owe your salespeople the feedback and training to ensure they succeed. You can always provide people feedback, but, if you are too new to provide them training, then you need to find someone who can, such as the sales training department or a field sales trainer.

Sometimes, because you have a track record of being a great manager, you may get a job as a manager at another company. There, you may be managing people who sell products you know very little about. First, you MUST go through the sales training yourself. Many new managers don't take the time or the effort, assuming they will learn it as they go. You are doing yourself and your team a disservice.

Second, early on, if you have poor performing or new salespeople, you must step up and find someone to give them the training they need, even if you must pay a customer an honorarium to help train them, DO IT!

In summary, the FVL is the most powerful legal document you have to protect yourself and the company as well as give sales people the feedback they deserve. Do them!!

- ◆ **Planning and Goals** – New or struggling salespeople often need a plan of attack and written goals. There is no doubt that written, specific goals, backed by a burning desire, create a powerful path to success. The struggling salesperson who doesn't seem to be responding to your verbal direction will rapidly begin responding when you put it in writing. New salespeople often need direction and guidance. By including clear, concise direction in their FVLs, you will help them immensely.

FVLs are also excellent ways to re-emphasize verbal direction you or the company may be communicating. The VP of sales may get up at the kickoff national sales meeting and proclaim, "This year, our emphasis will be on new products." In your division meeting breakout at the end of the week, you may reiterate that in your final rally speech, "This year, we must follow the direction of the VP and sell new products." But if during your first FVL you mention nothing about where the sales reps stand on new products, whether good or bad, you are failing to drive home the importance of selling "new products." The FVL is a great place to re-emphasize all the verbal direction and emphasis both you and the company are giving, but now in written form.

- ♦ **Communication** – You may not particularly like a certain sales representative, but you must still communicate with him/her. It can sometimes be very difficult with some salespeople. They might be overly defensive, irritating, or constantly combative. By setting the standard with all your salespeople, whether good or bad, that you will be doing FVLs with everyone, it will come as no surprise when you e-mail one of your difficult people his/her FVL. Whether the rep likes it or not, you are opening a line of communication between yourself and the rep.

Some companies don't require FVLs from their managers, but that doesn't mean you shouldn't be doing them. You need to let your region director or the VP/director of sales (your immediate superior) know that you will be doing FVLs for both the good salespeople and the bad salespeople and will copy them. This opens up the lines of communication between you and your mentor and lets them know what areas you are working on with each of your people. That way, if one of your reps decides to call your manager or HR directly to complain (backdoors you), you will have been keeping your mentor well informed as to the issues and problems the sales rep is having. There will be no surprises, and you will hopefully get the support of your mentor.

On a positive note, it also is a great way to again bring recognition to the sales reps for the good things they are doing. It can be very motivational.

17

HOW TO PREPARE FOR THE FIELD VISIT

♦ **What are your goals and the representative's goals for your field travel?**

THIS SHOULD BE COMMUNICATED WITH the sales representative prior to your arrival, at least a week prior to your visit. It's usually not good to spring your objectives on the reps the night before. Try to spend three solid days with a rep each field visit, but there are no hard-set rules. Be flexible. You may want to be in a territory Tuesday through Thursday, but you may be needed Monday through Wednesday or even through Thursday.

As time goes on, you will find there are some reps you just can't bear to spend three days with. You'll have to break up the time. Work with one rep two days and another rep two days, or spend two days on the road with the unbearable rep and maybe a day in your hometown working with the local rep.

You might be asking yourself, "Why don't you just get rid of the unbearable reps if they are that bad?" Sometimes even good reps are hard to be around for three days. You can't fire someone because you don't enjoy being around him for three days. You might also ask, "Well, if he is unbearable to me, is he probably unbearable to customers?" Maybe "unbearable" is too strong a word. Not many customers have to spend three-straight days with a sales rep. Remember, "Success comes in many forms." Haven't you ever seen a rep who wins awards every year, and you ask yourself, "How in the world does he do it with that personality?" Maybe you haven't, but keep an open mind and be flexible.

There is one exception to the rule of advanced notice. Unfortunately, there will come a time when you suspect a sales representative has just quit working, is doing something unethical, or could even be working another job. Sometimes it happens abruptly, and if he/she has been a poor-performing rep, you have every right to call the rep last minute and let him/her know you are coming to work with the person. If he/she is working hard and doing everything on the up and up, why should the rep care? It is the one who is off selling real estate or sleeping until 10 a.m. that usually becomes defensive.

Out of courtesy for your great reps or even your average reps, you should give a few days' notice that you are coming to town. Because a lot of salespeople have pride in what they do, they want to be extra prepared, with backup plans in case things fall through.

What we have found over the years is that the great reps often give you an open invitation to come to work with them last minute, anytime. Not only do they look forward to your visits, knowing that they often close even more business during your visits (tag-team approach), but they also know the importance of bringing "a suit" around to visit key customers. They know that great customers want to be made to feel important and special. They are also the same salespeople who are constantly asking the region director and VP/director of sales to come visit their territory any time. They have nothing to hide and relish your visits and corporate brass visits.

You know you have a performance problem on your hands when a sales rep comes up with a million excuses the day before your field visit. "My dog died." "I'm sick." "My grandmother just passed away."

Listen to your gut concerning your salespeople; often it will be right. If your gut is telling you someone isn't working, he/she probably isn't. Sometimes we ignore our gut feeling because we don't want it to be true or we don't have the time to deal with it.

♦ **Do your reps have marketing tools, demos, sales brochure binders, etc. with them?** Never let your salespeople work without detail bags, demo kits, etc. Sometimes your reps may stop off for "a minute" to drop something off to a customer or to leave a brochure. Never let them run in without their tools. Too many times, that one customer they've been trying to see for weeks just happens to be walking out of his/her office. Many selling opportunities are missed because the sales rep thinks, "I'll just be in there for a minute, and I don't feel like dragging everything in." Great reps are always prepared and ready to sell.

♦ **Pre-call plan prior to each call with rep.** What is the objective of each call? This is important for the rep to know but also for the manager to avoid "foot in mouth" disease. If you are both on the same page, then your goals are aligned. How many times has a manager opened his/her mouth only to destroy the tactic a rep might be trying to deploy? How many times do VPs of sales, managers, or region directors go into sales call, and like a big shot they give away the farm or make promises they can't or won't ultimately keep? The salespeople know the accounts, know the customers, and by having a discussion prior to the call, they can align everyone as to the objective of the call.

By the same token, many poorly performing salespeople will have no objective or goal for the call. By having the discussions before every call, you can help develop that person into the habit of having an objective for every sales call. Customers don't like random "drop-ins" with no objective. They are busy. If you are going to drop in, have a purpose.

♦ **Let the rep make the call, not you.** This is a good rule of thumb, but don't take it to the extreme and allow the sales representative to lose an opportunity or, worse, lose existing business. Your visit is a great opportunity to allow your salespeople to make mistakes and learn. However, we believe that if they get off track, as an experienced sales representative and manager, you owe it to their livelihood, the company's, and yours to step in without embarrassing anyone.

Sure, if your sales rep is merely making a presentation or demo on a single product, by all means let him/her have at it. But should the rep bring you into a negotiation that could lead to substantial amounts of growth dollars or a negotiation to maintain a large base of business, do not let him/her jeopardize either.

The main purpose is to never overpower a sales call. You might add a comment here or there, but don't open the discussion, don't lead a discussion, and don't close a discussion. Sometimes salespeople even complain that their managers never say anything in sales calls. Don't be an empty suit either.

———◆———

Dave:

Many years ago, I had a new sales representative take me into an account without any prior planning or solid objectives. I let him get away with this hoping to be able to coach him AFTER the call. The call went like this: We walked into the hospital and up to the operating room. We had a short talk with the buyer. The buyer started showing immediate signs of needing some of our products without ever really asking. However, my representative was so concerned (and maybe nervous that I was with him for the first time), he wasn't listening very carefully. He totally missed out on what might have been a huge purchase order.

We left the department and headed toward the car when I promptly stopped him and asked him to sit down with me in the lobby to discuss the call. I asked what he felt he had done well and what could have been improved upon. He felt like the call went great and thought that the next time he was in the account he could close some new business.

At this point, you probably already know where I am going. I asked him why he didn't attempt to close on this call. The buying signals were there, and he came to realize this once we went through a brief overview of the call. Again, he said he would "try" to get the order next week when he was back in the account. Then he made the biggest mistake of his young career. He said, "The account was not ready to buy." Needless to say, I challenged him and asked him to go back up to the operating room while I waited in the lobby. My simple instruction to him was this: don't come back down until you get the order TODAY. Normally I would never put that much pressure on anyone, but clearly the buyer was ready to give us an order had we simply asked.

Without having to say more, he scurried off to the elevator and went back to the buyer. Thirty minutes later a smiling young professional stepped off of the elevator with a purchase order in hand along with a confident strut. He told me the buyer was indeed ready to place an order today and was shocked that the representative had not "asked" for the order.

The moral to the story:

♦ Have a pre-call planning session BEFORE every call and a plan of action.

- Sometimes you have to encourage or even force your reps out of their comfort zones by pushing them. Insisting that my salesman go back to the buyer and not come back until he had a purchase order was a great lesson.

- Finally, and most important of all: Never, ever, make a decision for your customer. This rep had in his mind that this account was not ready to place an order. Why? Was it a lack of confidence that he would fail in front of me? Maybe. Lack of closing skills? Maybe. Lack of listening skills? Most certainly.

My Paul Harvey "The Rest of the Story" rendition: Not only has this young sales professional gone on to be a huge success, but he is now VP sales for a HUGE medical device firm. We stay in touch quite frequently and laugh about that call that took place many years earlier.

———◆———

- **Post call discussion on how the call evolved.** This is critical. You must review the call and openly discuss how the call went and discuss agreed-upon objectives and action steps to take to either take the next step in the sales cycle or to close the business. You can't put anything in a field visit letter if you didn't take the time to discuss it during the field visit. That would be an easy way out. First, if you are willing to put something positive in a field visit letter, why not tell the representative in person? Second, the same hold true for any constructive feedback.

- **Follow up with an FVL – NO Surprises.** Finally, now that you have told the team you will be doing FVLs, you must actually sit down and spend the five to 10 minutes to actually do the FVL after each field ride. If you don't, you will become the average manager who says one thing and does another. With all facets of being an exceptional manager, you must "do what you say and say what you do." The fastest way to lose respect of your team is to constantly make statements, promises, or requests and not follow up.

Also, salespeople, or human beings for that matter, don't like being surprised. Don't spend three days with someone, all smiles and fun, and then hit him square in the eyes with a FVL full of criticism. Always remain a caring individual. If you have a problem with a sales rep, visit with him/her, express your concern, lay out your expectations and the action plan you expect, and follow up with an FVL outlining your discussion.

All your communication, both verbal and written, should maintain a consistent and professional pattern. "No surprises" is one of the rules to follow.

Dean:

When I first became a manager, I had a sales representative who really felt he was one of the great sales reps of all time. He did not take constructive coaching well but desperately needed it. He also seemed to be someone who could be dangerous if backed into a corner. The best way to handle someone like this is to document everything. Verbally have discussions and then be sure to send a field visit letter. During the first few months, I rode with him and failed to give him any verbal or written feedback. After the year was up, I had to do his annual performance review. My conscience would just NOT let me let him slide. I wrote a very thoughtful review and pointed out all the good things about him and his performance as well as the things he needed to improve. When we went over the review verbally, it did not go well. He was incredibly defensive and asked for a specific example of my "accusations" as he put it. It became somewhat confrontational, even though he knew I was right.

The mistakes I made that I never made again were 1) I didn't provide him feedback throughout the year, both verbal and written, not only after each call but in summary FVLs, and 2) I didn't provide specific examples of his behavior and areas that needed improvement. As an example, don't just tell someone he/she needs to ask more open-ended questions. After a field visit, site examples in which the rep did not do this and then follow it up with a written field visit letter. Also, don't forget to site things the rep is doing well.

18

DOS AND DON'TS FOR THE FIELD VISIT

DOS

> - Set expectations with the representative and theirs of you
>
> - Have a pre-call plan
>
> - Listen to and observe the representative and customers
>
> - Have a post-call wrap up
>
> - Praise the representative early and often
>
> - Be honest with performance. Give constructive feedback on areas to improve
>
> - Follow up with commitments in a field visit letter
>
> - Discuss commitments from field visits and progress in weekly call-ins

DON'Ts

> - Make the call for the representative
>
> - Take over the call
>
> - Overshadow the rep in his/her account
>
> - Assume
>
> - Don't talk too much during the call

——◆——

Dean:

Dave and I are in absolute agreement on this point. Throughout my career, I haven't seen many successful managers who manage through intimidation. Maybe you are having success with it. Sure, there are certain "churn and burn" organizations that have always managed salespeople through intimidation and always will. It's not our approach, and, in the majority of situations, it is not an effective approach. Does that mean you can't demand performance and excellence? Of course not! We have had tremendous success by managing through a positive approach of coaching, mentoring, and developing. Does that mean that when someone just doesn't care or isn't doing his/her best that we sit around and allow the person to continue indefinitely? No, it doesn't. It's just a matter of approach and technique.

——◆——

Dave:

Please make sure your representative feels good about himself/herself after a field visit or a particular call. Do not manage through intimidation. Be an encourager. Be a cheerleader. Coach. Discuss things that went well and things that could be improved. Ask how he/she feels. Get to know each rep. Let your team see that you care. Be there for each member of your team.

19

THINGS TO DISCUSS DURING THE FIELD VISIT

1. ACCOUNTS TO BE VISITED.

2. Territory/Account trends – You and your sales reps should be reviewing sales trends on a monthly basis. Before your visit, you should review numbers for glaring positive and negative trends.

3. Budget – Review trends to forecast/budget both sales and expenses.

4. Focus or high-profit margin products – In order to maintain profitability as well as R&D, reps must sell focus products. Be prepared to discuss the trends in this area.

5. Current promotions – Selling focus products and participating in promotions are not options. Companies provide promotions not only as additional incentive for sales reps, but also to encourage sales reps to focus on products the company needs people to spend time selling. Often salespeople and managers will complain that a company doesn't have a pipeline of new products. This is the reason it is imperative for sales reps and managers to focus on new products. They are what drive profit, R&D, and acquisitions of new products.

6. Customer training and development – This is a major way to drive relationships and product utilization for the long term.

7. Discuss targets and next steps – This is imperative.

8. Other opportunities.

9. Discuss business plans and action steps

10. Territory management skills

11. Sales skills

12. End the field visit with positive feedback.

20

POST CALL AND FIELD VISIT DISCUSSIONS

POST CALL QUESTIONS:

> What did we accomplish?

> If you were making the call again, what would you do differently?

> What have you learned that will influence future calls on this account or customer?

> What have you learned that you can use elsewhere?

Remember...

> High Achievers want quick feedback.

> High Achievers want to know where they stand.

> High Achievers value commission $$$.

Dean:

Pre and post call discussions can sometimes be uncomfortable, but you've got to do them even with tenured salespeople. Don't walk into a sales call blind. Discuss what you want to accomplish on the call before going into the call. The best time to have a post call discussion is immediately after the call, not two days later.

Dave:

The post call "interview" is imperative. It sets the tone for the long-term success OR failure of this representative. Winners are waiting for feedback. The average guy/gal just goes about his/her day. Really ask yourself after each call, "How is my representative acting AFTER the call?" If he/she just wants to talk about crazy things that had nothing to do with the call, you may consider that to be a red flag. Not always, just consider it. However, if the rep starts asking, "What do you think? How do you think that call went?" you've most likely got yourself a winner!

As always, make the person feel good about himself or herself. The sales call may not have gone the way you wanted or the rep wanted, but after carefully coaching, listening, and giving feedback and direction, you are closer to having another winner on your team.

21

FORMAT OF A FIELD VISIT LETTER

Section A: Year to date sales results

YOU DON'T HAVE TO GET too complicated on a field visit letter. For the most part, it can be brief and to the point. For the reps who are doing well, a quick summary of the week is all that's needed. For a struggling rep, the FVL may be a little more difficult to write, but you should have a standard format for each FVL.

The first section should be a summary of where the sales rep stands year to date with sales. Cut and paste from your sales reporting system where the rep stands year to date against forecast, against last year's sales, % increase YTD, and dollar growth YTD. If you are in a growth, startup type mode, quarter over quarter and month over month sales is vitally important. Sales against the prior year may not be as relevant because last year each territory may have averaged $10,000 a month and this year you may be trending at $70,000 a month

You might also include YTD rankings within your region/district and YTD rankings nationally, if you can. Most reps enjoy and want recognition. They want to know where they stand, so if you or the company doesn't send out rankings, you are making a mistake. Reps love rankings unless they are in the bottom half. They are tremendously self-motivating.

At the bottom of the first section of the FVL, include a summary paragraph summarizing sales YTD, complimenting the rep on a job well done, encouraging the rep if he/she is in the middle of the pack, or pointing out poor performance if the rep is scraping the bottom of the barrel.

Section B: Current targets as observed during field ride

After each sales call, you should discuss the sales opportunity just observed and the key agreed-upon action steps necessary to close the opportunity. You should list three to five main targets observed, listing the main parts that make up that target. What are they?

1) The opportunity.

2) The dollar amount the opportunity represents.

3) What's in it for the rep? Commission dollars.

4) Who can make it happen? Name the key customer or other key drivers.

5) What is the next step to move the sales process along?

6) What action steps must be taken to close the deal?

7) What is the target date to close the sale?

You must get individual buy from the sales rep and agreement on these things. Here is an example:

1) Convert Dr. Zhivago at Czar Memorial over to Heart Valves R-US.

2) 50 valves per year, at $4,000 a valve = $200,000 per year.

3) 10% commission = $20,000

4) Dr. Zhivago and Nurse Ratchet, the OR materials coordinator who orders the products, are the two main contacts who can help you convert this business. Also, his private nurse in his office holds the key to his moods, his hours, his idiosyncrasies, his likes, his dislikes. Of course, he is the one who will demand your valves.

5) You need to take the request form that Dr. Z. filled out for your valves to Nurse Ratchet and ask her to place the order.

6) Get the sales rep to list the action steps necessary to close the deal.
   Actions Steps:

   ♦ Bring request form to Nurse Ratchet
   ♦ Get purchase order number.

- Get pricing approved and in the system.
- Place order with customer service or ensure Nurse Ratchet does.
- Get Dr. Zhivago's preference cards changed on the computer.
- Do in-service training for all OR shifts. Ensure order comes in.
- Ensure spot is cleared on the shelves.
- Be there for first six cases with Dr. Zhivago.

7) Agree on a close date to have the product stocked on the shelf and being used. March 31, 2008

Section C: Strengths

Talk about all the things the sales rep is doing well. Be generous in this section. Describe the sales calls and what you appreciated about the rep's technique/ abilities.

Section D: Areas for improvement

Some managers make the mistake of unloading on a sales representative with 20 things he/she needs to improve. Granted, some salespeople need a lot of work, and it can be very frustrating when there are so many things you'd like to change. Just pick out the two most powerful things the person can do or change to impact the business the most. If you unload with all 20, the rep will feel as though you are just beating him/her up and probably will shut down. You will de-motivate the rep rather than motivate him/her. Basically, you will be sending a message that the rep is horrible. Now if it's someone you would like to see leave the company, maybe you do list all 20 things, but be careful. If performance is average, but acceptable, then you may cause yourself a lot of problems. If performance is poor, and you've been documenting behavior and performance all along, maybe you do want to "unload" on the rep.

Basically, you should be riding with each sales rep at least once a quarter, and each time you should be writing a field visit letter.

22

RECOGNIZING PERFORMANCE ISSUES

You can't escape the responsibility of tomorrow by evading it today.

- Abraham Lincoln

THE POINT HONEST ABE MAKES is that it is easy to hope that a poorly performing sales rep will just naturally pick up the pace, that whatever was bothering him/her clears up, or the person leaves the company. The reality is that in most situations, as long as you let someone slide and slack off, the rep will stay as long as you let him/her, bringing your team down all the while.

These are signs you may have a representative with performance issues:

1) **Sales numbers are declining** – this is the most obvious sign of performance issues. You need to be paying attention to the sales trends and reports of all your salespeople at least monthly, hopefully weekly, if not on a daily basis. If you follow the trends, you can quickly take action and get things turned around.

2) **New product sales are low, and the rep is focusing on easier, low-profit products**. The lifeblood of every company is new products. They are what drive the profit and bottom line as well as provide dollars for R&D. Many times, they are higher priced upgrades to existing products. They provide additional benefits, but often the old products can still be used. Many poorly performing salespeople refuse to sell these products because it is more difficult. If the majority of salespeople are selling new products, it isn't acceptable for some reps to not sell the new products. This is a performance issue that needs to be addressed.

3) **Excuse-makers who don't take responsibility for performance.** This is the sign of below-average sales reps and those you may not want "on your bus." At sales meetings and conference calls, they are always negative and complaining. They can really pull your team down. They have the "sky is falling" or "woe is me" mentality. They can be a real "disease" to not only your sales team but to the entire organization. They are always blaming everything and everyone else for their poor performance. They blame the company, you, the products, and even the customers. They usually fly by the seat of their pants and have no plan of attack. Ask them for a target list or goal list, and they won't have one.

4) **Poorly organized during field visits.** When you ride with poorly organized reps, they are all over the place. Again, they have no plan of attack. The few appointments they set usually cancel. They can't seem to get in to see customers, and when they do get in to see someone, they are unorganized. Their detail bag is missing half the things needed to properly execute an effective sales call.

5) **Seemingly no relationships with key decision-makers or support staff.** In fact, when you arrive at the accounts, the customers who do know them don't seem too excited to see the rep.

6) **Never seem to get administrative duties completed or in on time.** Every company has administrative tasks, whether it be expense reports or weekly/monthly reports, yet these people never get theirs done or they're always late.

7) **You never hear from them, and they avoid speaking to you.** Poor performing reps hope if they don't speak to you, their little secret of failure will remain a secret. This is why mandatory weekly call ins are a must. Every should understand why.

8) **Customers and internal support staff are complaining about them.**

9) **They constantly sell on price.**

Dean:

I had a sales rep during my last training assignment as a field sales trainer, who was probably THE most-negative sales representative I ever managed. He blamed all his failures on the company, the products, the territory, and his customers. You know when a salesperson is always speaking negatively about his/ her customers, there is usually a performance issue to follow. The real problem with this guy was that he didn't work hard. He had too many side projects going on, so to cover things up, he tried to blame everything and everyone else for his poor performance. If he had spent as much energy selling as he had complaining, he would have done all right.

23

GO WITH YOUR GUT AS WELL AS THE FACTS

Leaders are visionaries with a poorly developed sense of fear and no concept of the odds against them.
- Robert Jarvik, artificial heart inventor

WHEN YOU FIRST BECOME A manager or when you go to a new company to take over a team, you are going to get lots of feedback from your mentor, the manager before you, or some interim manager who was leading the team for a few months before the company hired you.

Your mentor may give you his/her advice as to what you need to do in the next few months, which might include firing or pushing a few reps out of the company. Take all the information, comments, suggestions, and feedback and process them but DO NOT MAKE ANY RASH DECISIONS. First, understand that we realize it can be intimidating. Your mentor is telling you to fire someone, and we are telling you to hold your horses. It can be frustrating because, in reality, the manager before you should have taken action and done the dirty deed, but he/she pushed it off. Now you are expected to be the bad guy. The VP or director of sales often takes the feedback from the prior manager or others, and the only people who truly understand the situation is the prior manager or the sales representative.

There are a few problems with your just starting a new position and immediately firing people: 1) It will not help you build trust within the team. They will view you as a "hatchet man" or a "yes" manager, and they will possibly begin doing things to protect themselves, including making you look bad, 2) There may be extenuating circumstances that the VP or director is not aware of, or 3) There could have been a problem with the former manager, not necessarily the sale rep in question.

The point here is that you need to make a thorough assessment of the situation before you start chopping heads. Your goals, initially, are to fill any open territories and begin building a team. Developing or firing your weak links will come in time; and of course, you can't wait too long. Everyone must be pulling their weight.

———◆———

Dean:

During one management assignment, upon arriving on the job at the end of January, the director of sales proclaimed, "You have two weak links on your team and in order to have a great year, you should consider getting rid of both of them." He wasn't forcing me to do so, but I could tell he wanted me to move fast and to strongly consider it.

What I did do fast was get out in the field with both of them. The one rep was a good person but hadn't had a manager for seven months. So, instead of seeking direction from someone else, he decided just not to work. When we rode together, no one seemed to know who he was, especially the key customers. He also took it upon himself to tell me about all the real estate deals he was working on.

So, I laid out a plan for him to begin getting into surgery and put him on notice that he needed to start hitting plan. I went back to work with him two weeks later and saw that not much had changed as far as his work ethic. So, I put him on a performance plan and told him that I was not looking to fire him, but I needed him to begin hitting his monthly forecast. When I've had to put people on performance plans, I have always clearly set out obtainable objectives, and I work to help them hit those objectives. I take firing someone very seriously. It can destroy people's lives so I never take it lightly. I've known managers who have come into new assignments and didn't think twice about cutting half the team. I'm a big believer in "karma" so I always tried to give people the benefit of the doubt. On the other hand, if someone doesn't respond or acts belligerently, I move forward quickly to remove the rep from the company. If the rep doesn't put out the effort or doesn't want help, I would terminate the person at the end of the 90 days. In most cases the person left before I needed to do that. In the case of this guy, he actually began hitting forecast and began getting into surgeries. Unfortunately, he couldn't take the heat and ended up leaving the company.

In the case of the other sales representative, it turned out his son had cancer and he had just gotten over cancer himself, amazingly enough. I verified this and made the decision to give him time to turn it around. We had a discussion, and I just told him that I needed his help to make it happen. Immediately his numbers began to rise, and he ended up in the top 10. Each year, his rank rose even higher so that by the time I left, he was ranked No. 2 or No. 3. I believe, even though he was initially put off by the fact that I even had a discussion surrounding performance, he came to appreciate my support and encouragement. I can tell you this: had my son had cancer at the same time I had cancer, I don't know how productive I would have been. I believe this person was incredibly strong to even stay at his job, and the manager prior to me should have been more supportive.

---◆---

Dave:

Dean is right on the money. One experience I had in this regard was with a salesperson who was an underachiever with a bad attitude. I had inherited this person and when meeting with me, he unloaded about all he had going on in his life. This guy had more problems in his personal life than I could ever imagine. However, what I found out is that no one in the company had cared enough to ask him what was going on. Others just assumed his performance and attitude were poor because he wasn't working and didn't care. Actually, it was quite the opposite.

At the close of our field visit, I told him that I cared about him and only wanted the best for him and his family. He was given two choices: 1) Either he needed to turn it around and start hitting forecast on a routine basis, or 2) Begin looking for another job.

Much to my surprise, he called me the next day and asked me for 90 days as he had decided to find another career. We agreed at that moment that I was going to begin interviewing for his territory, and that I would "protect" him for 90 days. Somewhat uncommon, but in the best interests of helping a young man having a tough time and the need to fill a territory with a superstar, it worked.

Managers need to have empathy and listen. Your direct reports want to talk with you. They want to tell you about what is going on in their lives. I make it a practice that on all field travels, one night I take the whole family to dinner or at least the spouse/significant other. It allows me to tune into what is going on behind the scenes. It is amazing to befriend new people and watch them push their spouses to be successful.

---◆---

Dean:

One more recent example: I had a rep working for me who, through no fault of his own, kept being assigned new territories by the consulting company used each year to determine expansion, etc. He would literally be assigned completely new customers each year. He lived in Orange County, so one year he had part of the OC and the desert, then he had northern OC, East LA, and Downtown, then he had Long Beach, the South Bay up through Santa Monica. I really liked this guy's sales approach. He was one of the best challengers I had ever seen. He'd get things rolling and then the change. My prior two sales directors were supportive, but a new one came in, looked at the early numbers in the year, and quickly wanted me to fire him. I didn't, which put me at odds with my mentor, but year after year after that mentor was fired, this guy performed in the top 10% of the sales rankings. He just needed a place to call home for a while. I've very proud of him. As a manager, you can run into challenges like this with your mentor. You've got to try and hold your ground for what you know to be the right thing. In the end, you will be alright.

---◆---

So, management isn't all about gut feel, and it isn't all about facts and numbers. It is a combination of the two. It's an art and a science. It is also about taking into consideration the moral and ethical implications of your decisions as well as how your decisions might affect the entire team. Imagine the loss of morale and support from the team had Dean terminated a guy whose son had cancer and who just gotten over it himself! What sort of respect would the team have had for him—not to mention the fact that it just wouldn't have been right? Sometimes, you must make decisions that will not sit well for the team, but that is the right thing to do for them, overall, and for the company. But, be very careful about acting merely on the request or advice of others until you study the facts for yourself.

24

BE A GOOD LISTENER

I have learned the novice can often see things that the expert overlooks. All that is necessary is not to be afraid of making mistakes, or of appearing naïve.
- Abraham Maslow, psychologist

AS IT IS WITH BEING a great salesperson, in order to be successful as a manager, you need to be a good listener. It is a major part of your job. You need to hear what your customers are telling you, what your salespeople are telling you, what your superiors are telling you, what marketing is telling you, and what the company is telling you. By really listening, you can put together a successful action plan to make your team winners. Miss one of the data points, and you may fail.

Many times, managers may make the mistake of only listening to what the company/superiors are telling them, while they could be receiving tremendous market information from their reps. Sales reps are on the front lines and more than anyone else in the company, they have their fingers on the true pulse of the customer. Yes, sometimes they tend to overact and want to make rash decisions, but it is your job to listen to the information they are providing, decipher it, and communicate it in a positive way to marketing and upper management. If one of your poorly performing reps is overreacting, then maybe you wait a bit. But if you are getting the same data on a certain issue from all your team, include it in your monthly report in a positive manner. If one of your top-performing reps communicates something, you should certainly take note. You should take note of all your reps' communication and comments, but if a higher performer gives you feedback, it means more than information coming from your lowest-performing sales rep. As a manager, listening is probably the most important trait you can bring to your team. The respect that you earn is due in large part to your listening skills and desire to want to help others. Do you want to lead? You'd better listen first. Do you want to coach? You'd better listen first. Do you want to build a team? You'd better listen first. Do you want to build rapport and respect? You'd better listen first.

We love to say, "Tell me what's going on." Very open-ended, but it allows your salesperson to open up. If you don't think he/she is telling you what is really going on, push it one step further. Ask, "Now tell me . . . what is *really* going on"? The emphasis on *really* says to the rep that you know there is more. Listen carefully, show that you care, coach if the time is right. Put action steps in place if performance is what is *really* on the rep's mind.

Listen, listen, listen!!

Dean:

One of the ways to get the best out of people as individuals and as a team is to listen. If your reps have concerns about the company, the comp plan, the forecast, or any other issue, you had better listen. If you want your people to run through walls for you, they better have your ear. You may not be able to fix everything or change the course of the company, but if your reps believe you listen to them, and you go to bat for them, they will respond positively. Too many managers are afraid to address the concerns of their team with upper management. They don't want to rock the boat. It's like anything in life; if you do things in a positive, digestible manner and provide potential solutions, usually upper management or your mentor will listen.

Dave:

This has saved me many times. Let me explain. Taking the time to get to know your direct reports and their families really helps endear them to you. A trust is built, and when another job opportunity arises for my top performers, on many occasions over the years these guys/gals would come to me to discuss those opportunities before leaving. I firmly believe in setting the tone early on with all of my new hires so that if something else comes along that might seem better and more suited to them, they'll give me a chance to discuss it before making a final decision. Time and time again, after discussing with my folks, they realize what they currently have is "much greener" than they thought.

Some might question this as a lack of loyalty that someone would look around or even entertain the thought of leaving. Why? Wouldn't you look or at least be flattered if something you felt was more challenging came along? Of course, you would. We are people with feelings, families to support, and we all long for more money and responsibility. However, most of these new opportunities that come along are not very good at all. However, it takes trust and listening to discover the "hot buttons" that your representative is exploring. Once you know this, it's much easier to "sell" your organization. Trust and listening skills are paramount, and all of the best leaders possess these skills.

> *Courage is what it takes to stand up and speak. Courage is also what it takes to sit down and listen.*
> *- Winston Churchill, British prime minister who helped save the world.*

25

TECHNICAL OR CLINICAL PEOPLE IN SALES: IS IT GOOD?

YOU MAY HAVE YOUR OWN opinion about hiring technical or clinical salespeople, but we feel that nine out of 10 technical/clinical people don't make good salespeople. They certainly can hold a place within medical or pharma companies, but most don't end up being great sales reps. Now, keep in mind, if you happen to find a technical or clinical person who has done well in sales, they can be lethal, selling machines, but usually not. They believe they can do the job but never realize how tough it is. You will find most will perform at an average or below-average level. Usually you will find they don't have sales awards on their resumes. For us, a candidate with a clinical background would have to have been consistently "all-world" in sales at a prior sales job to be considered. Many technical or clinical people think that being a sales rep is going around handing out doughnuts and telling jokes. They don't realize the pressure. That is why many return to nursing or are laid off. When companies have layoffs, they usually keep the best reps, not the clinical or technical support people.

That's a harsh paragraph. We love nurses and OR techs. They helped both of us get to where we are today. We also need them out there advocating and caring for patients. We need technical people out there keeping the world working. They can be your best allies in a hospital, and the same goes true for technical staff in companies you may call on. People can learn to become sales people, and great sales people at that, but when hiring for that all-important opening that you have, which will elevate your team to the next level of success, you might not consider a clinical or technical person UNLESS they have already proven they are a top 10 sale rep.

Now, we did say nine out of ten. So, for those of you technicians, RNs or former PAs who have gone on to be stellar representatives, please understand, we know you are out there and we respect your accomplishments. In fact, those who are part of the successful 10% are unstoppable because they can combine their clinical/ technical knowledge with their sales ability. This applies to any industry. Let's say that again, if you find an outstanding sales person with a clinical or technical background, they are lethal as they bring both salesmanship and the knowledge customers respect. But should you be the one to give a nurse, right out of nursing, his first sales job? Probably not. They'd be better off getting a job as a nurse educator, or clinical specialist inside a company, where they can prove to reps and managers that they have the drive and ability to sell.

———◆———

Dean:

When companies I've worked for announce they want to hire clinical people in the field to support the salespeople, I sometimes push back and ask if they would just let me hire a junior rep who can sell. I understand the whole theory that "doctors and nurses will often listen to their peers more than salespeople," but I have worked with many sales professionals who had the respect and the ear of many medical professionals; those health care providers listened to their advice and input. Those are the types of reps I want to hire or have hired.

———◆———

Dave:

Well said. Bottom line: give me a selling machine any day of the week. Over a period of time, my selling machine will be up to speed clinically enough to earn the respect of the physicians and techs the rep serves.

———◆———

Now, with the Affordable Care Act, and access to doctors decreasing for pharmaceutical reps, many companies have moved to hiring many nurse educators, etc. as a way to get access, information, and a message across. This can work, and it is working in the pharmaceutical industry. One thing everyone in an organization needs to understand is that companies are in business to sell and move products.

Yes, they absolutely want to help patients with new technology, but what keeps the lights on in the buildings is selling product. We love nurse educators and medical scientific liaisons, but they have to understand why they are there in the first place.

26

MANAGE EACH PERSON INDIVIDUALLY

*The job of the manager is enabling, not a directive job.
Coaching and not direction is the first quality of leadership
now. Get the barriers out of the way to let people do the things
they do well.*

- Robert Noyce, founder, Intel

ONE OF THE FIRST AND biggest mistakes a rookie manager will often make is trying to manage everyone the same. Often the reason it happens is: 1) No one gives the new manager any training. He/she is a top sales representative, and the company plucks him/her out of the field to manage a sales team. 2) Because the new manager was successful as a sales rep, their belief is that to be a great manager and to lead the team, he/she just needs to make everyone a great sales representative just like them. Inexperienced managers fail to recognize that there are many ways to success.

We've mentioned over and over again that drive and passion are the most important ingredients for every great representative, but some managers fail to realize that it comes in many forms and styles of selling.

Some representatives are driven by commission dollars and couldn't care less about awards. Some reps live for the pat on the back from the manager and recognition in front of peers at national meetings. For this group, commissions are secondary.

Some salespeople are more reserved but win awards and earn top commissions through their honesty, integrity, and hard work. Others are the life of the party and the best storytellers around. Great reps come in many forms. Everyone is motivated by slightly different things. Understand your individual salespeople, manage them separately and differently, and you should do well. Try to force people to conform to your way, and you will have a lot of turnover and will likely fail. But the two common threads that successful reps possess is drive and being challengers. So, while you must manage each rep individually, look for those two traits always.

———◆———

Dean:

When I first became a manager, I wrote down all the things I liked about my former managers, and all the things they did that I didn't like. I recognized the fact that some things they may have done were for my own good, so I crossed those off the list. The things that remained, I always tried to avoid doing when I was a manager and the thing my managers did well, I tried to incorporate in my approach. You remember the "Golden Rule"? It can apply in many facets of your life. It's like the dad who verbally abuses his son constantly, and the son says, "I'm never going to do that to my kid." What often happens? He forgets and does the same thing to his kid. Treat your people as you would like to be treated. Even if you must take corrective action, treat them with respect.

———◆———

Dave:

Ask your sales professionals what motivates them. Now that they've told you what gets them going every day, manage toward that direction. If it's money, challenge them every month to exceed forecast. Show them that if they do, the impact of exceeding forecast will positively impact their bank account. If it's recognition, point out to your team every chance you get how well this individual is doing (without overdoing it). Send e-mails to your mentor about the great things this person has achieved and cc: your representative. This will fire them up! Ask and listen.

27

HOW TO SAVE A TOP REP FROM LEAVING THE COMPANY

Anybody who runs a company has to have the capacity to sell, and sell well. You may be trying to sell the image of your company or selling employees on the idea of working hard, but it's all salesmanship. You can't turn your back on that part of the job.
    - William Kelly, chairman, Semi-Specialists of America

IN OUR CURRENT WORLD OF massive layoffs and jobs going overseas, many people feel that companies only care about the bottom line. They sense they are sometimes treated like pawns in a chess game, played and dispensed of in the stroke of an accountant's pen. Unfortunately, people no longer join companies with the thought of spending 20 or 30 years with them. Their outlook for a job is two to five years and then on to the next company that can pay more. There's a feeling in America that people need to get "their piece of the pie" before a company pulls the rug out from under them.

As a frontline manager, how do you build loyalty and how do you save sales representatives from leaving the minute another company offers another $25,000 a year? Turnover is incredibly costly and will slow you down from achieving your goals of success and commission. Once one of your best representatives leaves the company, the competition will be all over open territories and accounts pleading, "Hey, Theresa is gone. I've been patiently waiting. How about giving me a shot now?" You will not only have to spend a lot of time recruiting, interviewing, and hiring, but you will now have to cover the accounts and the problems yourself. All this takes away from developing and training your people as well as helping them negotiate and close large chunks of business.

As we've stated before, there are a lot of effective management styles that can work, depending on the type of company and products you represent. Management by intimidation has never been our style, and we have both been effective managing salespeople in entry-level roles as well as more advanced technical roles. That doesn't mean we don't react immediately to correcting poor performance or attitudes. It just means that we tend to manage in an atmosphere of fairness, positive thinking, and good business acumen. Again, let us state that you may not agree with every point in this book, but if you read with an open mind, you might pick up new strategies that will help you become a better manager. With commissions often making up 50% of your total compensation, as a manager, how your people perform directly affects how much money you make and how much recognition you will receive. Put your people first and the rest will come.

We're not saying that you shouldn't protect the interests of the company, just understand that your salespeople are, in a sense, your customers as well as your employees. Yes, you may have to be the tough guy sometimes, but if you manage fairly, when the hammer comes down the employee will know it is coming and usually will understand that he/she was deserving of being let go.

The following are long-term strategies for keeping good people, the steps we believe will help you keep top sales representatives from leaving the company. Some of these are repetitive from other chapters but important enough to repeat. Understand, however, that inevitably you will get that dreaded phone call in which one of your best reps announces he/she is leaving. Here's what we suggest you do:

Long-Term Strategies for Keeping Top Salespeople:

1) **Manage consistently and fairly with everyone.** This is more of a long-term strategy to help avoid good people from turning in their resignation, period. Don't manage everyone the same and understand that each person is motivated by something different.

2) **Analyze the individual situation of each representative for yourself** and don't just react to what your manager thinks is the right course of action. He/she may be right but also may not have enough information, which so often happens.

3) **Don't stand in the way of your people being promoted**. If you are a good manager, you will not be afraid of your people being promoted. In fact, you will help develop them so they can be promoted if that is what they want. Great managers have the confidence to know that they can hire another great sales representative right behind the one who was promoted. If your people know that you want the best for them, their careers, and their family, you will again build tremendous loyalty.

Poor managers are afraid to lose people to promotion. Many times, they didn't hire their best people and are concerned they won't be able to replace them. People can also be selfish and worry about their pocket first and the livelihood of their people second. Take care of your people first, and they will take care of your pocket by being the best they can be.

4) **Fight for your people when they deserve it and be their voice**. Often, your top people leave the company because they want to be promoted, get a raise, and maintain certain accounts. They rely on you to communicate these goals and other issues to upper management. Too many new managers or weak managers are afraid to stand up for what is right or stand up for their people.

One of the exercises during the sales manager training classes at Johnson & Johnson was to have all future managers sit in a room and discuss and present why their sales representative should be considered for the next promotion. What they were teaching us is that it is expected of you as a manager to know your people, their strengths, and their weaknesses, and to be prepared to fight for them for that next promotion if they deserve it. There may be more than one solid candidate, but unless you are willing to present your people, who will speak for them?

Helping with promotions is just one area in which your sales representatives rely on you to represent them. Bonus, territory alignments, merit increases, and pricing issues are just a few more. This leads to our next point.

5) **Be fair to everyone in every way.** There is no doubt that in a sales team of five to twelve, there are going to be those you really like, those who are just OK, and those you don't really care for very much. Understand that some of your best salespeople sometimes are going

to be people you just don't like. I know it seems hard to believe, but it's true. Also, know that every once in a while, you are really going to like someone as a person, but he/she just won't perform up to their ability and unfortunately, as a manger, you are paid to do what you must do. The bottom line is you should always be fair and consistent so that no one can ever cry foul.

When an average or below-average salesperson converts some business, give him/ her recognition on a text or e-mail and copy your mentor on the message. Don't give all the recognition to your best people and don't always give them everything, or else you'll never get anything out of the other people.

However, there is a fine line in this approach. The topic of this chapter is how to maintain and sometimes save your best people. Sometimes managers, in an effort to be fair to everyone, overdo it to the point of not being fair to their best people. In the quest for being viewed as fair, they don't reward the best people enough for jobs well done. So, rule No. 6 is:

6) **Reward top performance.** When people convert chunks of business, make sure you give them recognition. Sometimes below-average salespeople will complain that "so and so" gets all the recognition. Your answer to that can be, "When you convert business or do something good, you'll get plenty of recognition." You need to be fair so that when average people close business or do a great job, you need to recognize them. As a manager, you've got to be able to balance the long- and short-term goals.

The point is that if you manage fairly, you will cause everyone on the team to respect you and perform at a higher level. Understand that as a manager, you will never have everyone like you on your team, nor should that be your goal. Your goal should be that they respect you and that you respect them as human beings.

Just like treating average people with fairness and recognition when they do well, you must be sure to treat your best people fairly too. If they are the ones converting a lot of business, you must give them the recognition they are due and not hold back.

When it comes to handing out merit increases, being fair doesn't mean that you give everyone the same merit increase. You MUST reward your best people with the highest merit increases.

If you are required to split up a great salesperson's territory due to expansion, allow him/her some input into the decision. You may not be able to give the rep all the accounts he/she wants (again, due to fairness), but by giving him/her some input into the matter, you show respect to the rep. For instance, both territories may need to have a flagship account, in your mind. You may decide just to give the new rep a small territory with not a lot of existing accounts, but the company might consider giving that person a guarantee to allow him/her to grow the territory to a point the rep can make a good living without the guarantee. If your company won't do that, you must make it possible for both people to make a living. So, when splitting the accounts, give your existing great rep the opportunity to voice his/her opinion. Let the rep know you have a tough decision and that he/she can't keep all of the great accounts. By making the rep a part of the process, you gain loyalty.

Today, in larger companies, they bring in consulting companies to create expansion territories, etc. but in smaller companies, you may have the ability to create territories. You are going to want to do it as fair as possible.

———◆———

Dave:

If you are just entering sales management, get ready! One day, when you least expect it (usually on a Friday), your phone will ring and one of your top producers will announce to you that he/she has accepted another position with another company. It's inevitable if you manage long enough.

———◆———

Let's say you've been fair, but due to some changes in your company, one of your best representatives gives a letter of resignation. How do you keep him/her? First of all, you've got to try. If you don't, the rep's gone. Many times, with a little work on your part, you can keep him/her. Here are some additional steps when you find yourself in emergency mode:

Short-Term, Emergency Strategies

DON'T PANIC! That's much easier said than done. However, you need to always be prepared in advance of this happening. If it hasn't happened to you yet, count your blessings.

Find out: "Why are you leaving?" Truly try to understand why a representative is leaving. You will hear clues as to how you can salvage this rep. Remember, "It ain't over till it's over."

Compensation

The answer to the "Why" question is usually the same. "I can make more money, and my chances for upward mobility will happen much quicker. Oh? Let's play this out.

If your representative is starting over at a new company, how could that alone ensure quicker upward mobility? In regard to compensation, ask this individual what the new company is promising or estimating he/she will make? Usually the answer is the same; the dollar amount may be different, but the income stated is based on someone hitting forecast: "I can make up to $150,000 annually if I make my forecast."

We'll that's great. However, there is one huge opportunity for you to salvage this person. Ask him/her, "What's the forecast?" When forced to try and save someone from potentially making a mistake, ask this question to get the person thinking.

Most of the time, the rep will have NO IDEA what the forecast will be. Even if he/she did, how does the rep know it is achievable? We've received phone calls over the years from previous reps that left wanting to come back. They realize they made a huge mistake, and, sadly, their old territories have been filled. Usually you wouldn't want to take someone back who has left. He/she would have to have been the best of the best, and even then, the company might not let you bring the person back. It's usually "not greener on the other side;" there are too many unknowns. Many surprises await the rep in that "open territory." Why is it open??

Potential remedies to the compensation blues: As a top rep, many times companies will throw the person an extra bone to get him/her to stay. Once again, as a manager, you must **find out the difference** then **go to bat for the person.**

Sometimes the difference may be $25,000. Many times, you can work out a retention plan that can take many forms. 1) It may be a flat guarantee, so that if the comp plan doesn't quite pay what it said it would, the company makes up the difference. Include some sort of performance incentive to ensure the rep doesn't go to sleep on the job. (i.e., the person must hit 90% of plan, etc.), 2) Give some sort of partial retention bonus up front and then the rest of the bonus after performance goals are reached. Sometimes you can get some upfront money as a retention bonus; $5,000 now and $5,000 at the end of the year. Again, it makes no sense paying up front if the rep may be planning to turn around and leave. By then the rough waters have subsided, the company is back on track, and everyone is happy. Keep in mind, many companies just won't pay retention bonuses so don't guarantee anything until its "guaranteed."

Once someone leaves a company, statistics show that if the person comes back, it is usually very short-lived. If you can get someone to stay, show that the company cares, and help the rep through some company challenges, then often he/she will stay for many years. These retention bonuses and incentives are not something you want to do often, but every once in a while, if strategically used, they can help the company through a tough time and help maintain business. Great salespeople are not easy to find, so you just don't want to lose your top people. It sends a bad message to the rest of the sales force.

Also, clearly understand what YOUR company stresses as "value-added" incentives to retain employees. Is it a pension plan that many companies no longer have but yours does? What is the new company's 401(k) structured? Are there stock options they are walking away from? Is the chance for upward mobility better elsewhere?

Make sure you go through these things with the sales rep to ensure he/she is factoring everything into the equation. Make sure the rep is comparing apples to apples.

The company changed the comp plan.

This is a derivative of the above section on compensation. People don't like change, and many times, when a company changes a comp plan, rumors spread through the grapevine and without truly understanding the new plan, people panic. They buy into miscalculations either they or investigators made and send negativity around the company. They get mad. They listen to complainers about how no one will make as much as last year. The reason this happens is that a lot of companies make the decision to really reward top performers and penalize those who don't hit forecast. Who are the ones who are usually complaining the most about the new comp plan? The average or below- average people who realize they won't make as much as they did last year for average or below-average performance. Thus, you must **clearly go through the comp plan** and show each rep that as a consistent top performer he/she will actually make more than he/she did last year. You must take the time to EXPLAIN THE CHANGES.

Now sometimes, the changes in the comp plan were bad changes, but usually if a quarter or six months go by and no one is earning any money and reps start heading for the door, the company will make adjustments. Encourage your best reps to remain on the ship; avoid a career mistake and try not to be a martyr. Things will usually improve.

Maybe the sales rep is bored and needs a new challenge.

Go to management for approval to gives a promotion or new responsibilities, like becoming a field sales trainer. Maybe he/she becomes a key account specialist. Maybe the rep becomes an assistant DM working with you to develop into a division manager. Find out what he/she wants to do with his career and see if new responsibilities would make the rep stay. Again, something like this may not and probably won't be possible but you must try. Inquire about it.

Is your rep feeling under-appreciated by the company?

In every "rack and stack" review meeting with upper-management, you have been raising the red flag that this great rep is a flight risk, yet upper management doesn't seem to hear you. The VP or director of sales needs to get on the phone (at a minimum) or fly out to see the rep and acknowledge that he/she has been a tremendous performer, and the company neglected to recognize it. Don't worry about the recognition. In the end, the rep will know it was you who went to bat for him/her, but coming from the director will show the company is finally realizing the rep's value.

The rep may feel there are no new products in the pipeline.

Arrange for a conference call with the director of R&D, the director of marketing, and anyone else who can shed light to the rep as to where the company is heading. Again, no new products may mean the rep is bored or feels he/she won't have the opportunity to earn the same amount of money. He/she may feel the heat from the competition that does have new products. It's not that the rep isn't confident in his/her ability to fight the competition, but through the battles and the new comp plan, the rep foresees losing income. You need to remind your rep that every company, no matter how great, will go through periods of slowdown and slumps but that the great reps will always be OK. Many sales reps leave companies for the next best thing, a new blockbuster product, only to find they are out of a job in six months. Remind them that if they become job hoppers, they could become unmarketable.

A mutual friend of ours has hung in there through thick and thin—through the toughest of times, and the best of times. Because of his loyalty for top performance, the company always takes care of him one way or another, and he has, on average, made a very, very good living. He will retire a very wealthy man. Many of his cohorts left at the first sign of a rocky road. Many of them went on to make a little more money that first year, but the bottom fell out of their new companies, and they made a lot less the following years. Our friend was with a very good company in a very competitive market. Through it all, he remained consistently great, and his customers and his company rewarded him for it. This is the message you need to communicate to your great rep who is thinking of leaving. Hang in there. Times will get better. **I'm behind you. The company is behind you and so are your customers.**

Ask your top-notch salesperson to give you a few days before giving a final answer.

Even if he/she has given a final answer, nothing is final. Please remember that!!Call in the cavalry if necessary. Get your mentor or the VP of sales involved in talking directly to this person.

Dave:

In one case, our VP of sales flew in, and we saved an employee from making a HUGE mistake. This representative still thanks us for not letting him leave! As a side note, this individual sales professional stayed on another 10 years. Enough said!

——◆——

What to do during those few days you have bought? **Is there anyone you know who has ever worked for the organization to which your superstar is considering jumping?** Let someone else win the rep back. You don't have to be the hero. The main thing is to save a great salesperson. Often the company for which the great rep is leaving is not as good as it appears; sometimes it is horrible.

Allow **your representative the chance to "save face."** Ensure him/her that considering alternatives is normal, especially when things are not going well. However, jumping ship to another organization is usually not the answer. Encourage him/her to stick it out. You and others will support the rep tremendously. Encourage the spouse of the rep, whom you have hopefully gotten to know, to give her/his spouse a different perspective on the idea of changing jobs. Make sure they have both fully considered all the ramifications of leaving the company.

Will you save all people? Absolutely not. However, know your people and know what your company has to offer that this other company may not. **Bring in the cavalry to save this person**.

You always need to **build a bullpen of talent** that you could hire in a few weeks' notice. You just never know when someone will make that phone call to tell you he/ she is leaving and there is nothing you can do to stop them.

Recognize and don't ignore the signs that someone may be at risk to leave.

If your gut is telling you that someone is considering leaving, you are probably right. React before the rep gives notice. Make sure you communicate to your manager and to upper management that you feel that you may have a potential problem. In the quarterly management meetings while ranking and discussing employees, express your concerns. Take action to save a rep before it is too late.

Getting the VP or director of sales to call and talk to the rep to see how he/she is doing often opens the dialogue. Giving a retention bonus before the rep feels undervalued can help—if that's a possibility. Getting some sort of bonus or recognition can often get people back on the path of feeling good about themselves and the company.

Opening dialogue and communication is always a good policy. If you suspect a rep might be looking for another position, pick up the phone and ask how he/she is doing. Be direct. What's bothering him/her? Get the rep talking. You might alleviate any fears or concerns before your rep takes definite action. Like a good marriage, you need to have open and honest communication.

Signs your rep may be at risk for leaving:

- You usually speak to him/her once, twice, or three times a week and all of a sudden, the rep quits calling.

- You hear rumors the rep is looking and feel the rumors may be true.

- You never used to find him/her in his/her office. Now you sense the rep is in the office more than in the field.

- You used to be able to call the rep at any time on his/her cell, and now you are never able to reach the rep. He/she used to call you back within an hour; now it takes all day. The rep is likely interviewing.

- He/she starts taking strange days off, which is very out of character for that individual. He takes a Monday here and a Friday there.

- Other reps ask you, "What's up with so-and-so?" They are sensing something is up with the rep, too.

- Numbers are sliding, and the rep in question is normally a solid, consistent, above- average performer.

- He/she formerly enjoyed having you ride in the field with him/her but now is making excuses.

- He/she normally does administrative work before anyone else but now is consistently late or doesn't do any at all, a sign the rep no longer cares.

- ◆ The rep asks you to cover a case, and the customer mentions he/she hasn't seen the rep in a while.

- ◆ He/she used to be very vocal, energetic, and an active participant in meetings. Now the rep doesn't say a word.

If you communicate well with your reps, you should know something is not right. They usually will let you know if they are unhappy about something, but sometimes even the reps you are close to blindside you. Look for the signs and don't live in denial.

Here are some additional thoughts to share with your employee who is considering leaving the company:

Like any business, there are good recruiters and bad recruiters. Unfortunately, some recruiters have no problem giving people bad advice on resumes, career moves, companies, and everything else. However, there are also many caring, concerned recruiters who are in it for the long term and believe that if they treat people with respect and concern, it will come back to them tenfold. The representative shouldn't listen to what one recruiter says about a company. He/she should do research and talk to other reps and customers. He/she should always find out why the last rep left.

As a manager, what do we say when people come to us panicked because times have gotten tough at the company, and they want to jump ship? Usually, unless it is a case of ethics or morality, you should advise them to take a deep breath and consider staying put. You see, no matter how great a company is, even a giant like Johnson & Johnson, Medtronic, or 3M will experience back orders, recalls, FDA warning letters, clinical failures, products scares, media hype, mature product lines, barrage of competitors, patent expirations, lack of new products in the pipeline, and every other type of challenge the world can throw at them. No company is immune to these issues. Every company has its challenges.

Advise your reps: 1) Make sure you don't become a job hopper. 2) If you insist on leaving, make sure it is for the right reason and not your need to make a point to the company. There are too many martyrs who commit career suicide in order to be the "hero of the sales force." 3) Take time to let the company work things out. The majority of companies don't want to hurt their employees. If there is a problem, give them time to fix it.

28

LEAD BY EXAMPLE

People never improve unless they look to some standard or example higher and better than themselves.
- Tyron Edwards, American theologian

IF YOU WANT YOUR SALES reps to work hard, then you need to work hard.

If you want them to always look and sound professional, you need to look professional and sound professional—knowing talk tracks, data, products, competition, and things about the company as good if not better than they do.

If you want to make sure your people don't sell on price, when they call you in for the big negotiation, don't cave in and offer up an unheard-of price.

If you'd rather they never or rarely give away free samples, don't cave in and give away the farm.

If you are teaching not to give up something in a negotiation unless something is given in return, then practice what you preach.

If you want your reps to be team players, then you had better be a team player with your fellow managers.

If you want reps to help each other, then you should lend a helping hand to them and to help other managers. Are you afraid to cover calls or cases for them? Will you go if needed to visit customers for them if reps are ill or on vacation?

If you want your reps to act ethically and morally, they had better never catch you doing something against the law or against company policy. Cheat on your expense reports, and it will be hard for you to look them in the eye and discipline them for cheating or fudging on their expense reports.

If you want your people to be positive and upbeat, be positive and upbeat.

If you want them to set written specific goals, then you should be able to present written, specific goals for yourself and the team at a moment's notice.

> *A leader is one who knows the way, goes the way, and shows the way.*
>
> *   - John C. Maxwell, author and speaker*

———◆———

Dean:

If your reason for wanting a management position is power, you'll never get people to follow you. You've got to be willing to roll your sleeves up, get into the trenches, and help your people fight in the heat of battle. Then they will follow your lead. Managers who sit in their home office drinking coffee will never be great leaders.

———◆———

Dave:

Your job as a manager is to be a counselor, coach, great listener, tremendous judge of talent, hard worker, deal with HR issues, march to the orders of upper management whether or not you support their decisions, hit forecast, manage your budget, give feedback, fight for your team, and work with demanding customers.

Are you starting to get the message??

The reason I bring all of this to your attention is that if you are not able to "keep all of the balls in the air as a juggler," management might not be for you. Being a leader means you will work hard toward perfecting all the traits listed, and many more. Your team expects you to lead. Are you up to the task?

———◆———

> *The speed of the leader is the speed of the pack.*
>
> *   - Yukon saying*

> *Of course, it's what we do that counts, not what we say. Therefore, I set an example through my actions, and I believe*

it is critically important to be consistent, predictable, and dependable.
       - Donald E. Peterson, past chairman and CEO, Ford

Men pay no heed to a dog that is always barking.
       - Margaret Clement

29

COMMUNICATE WITH YOUR PEOPLE

By definition, communication means two-way communication.
Insecure individuals don't like it. Bosses don't like it, but
leaders and innovators do like it.
- Mark Shepherd, past chairman, Texas Instruments

A STRONG LEADER WILL COMMUNICATE whether they have to deliver good news or bad news. Some managers will avoid having verbal discussions with their reps by merely slipping feedback into a voicemail or field visit letter. Don't take the easy way out. Sometimes we need to ask our employees, "What could I be doing differently, in your opinion, to help you more?" Showing that you care is not a bad thing. Asking your direct reports this type of question means you care about their opinions. Don't we all want to express how we feel when asked? We are all human, and we all make mistakes. Why not admit that and ask for help? For many, egos get in the way. Please don't let that happen to you!

Again, like any interpersonal relationship, even though you may be right about a topic, try to understand a different point of view. Like selling a good customer, if you understand where a representative is coming from, you can convince him/her your ideas and point of view are good.

———◆———

Dean:

Next to your spouse or significant other, you spend more day-to-day interaction with your salespeople than most others. If any great relationship is to last, there must be open, two-way communication.

Dave:

Communication. WOW. That's a big word. How do you use proper communication as a sales leader? Ask questions. Get your direct reports to talk. What are they thinking? Are they OK? What can I do to help each become more successful? Get to know your people on a more personal basis. You must care and be sincere about this.

30

SET SPECIFIC WRITTEN GOALS FOR THE TEAM

Obstacles are those frightful things you see when you take your eyes off the goal.

- Henry Ford

JUST LIKE A GREAT SALES representative should have specific, written goals, so should you. Set goals for your team and for what you would like to accomplish as a manager. If your goal is to be region manager of the year, break that goal down to action steps on an annual, monthly, weekly, and daily basis. How much converted business will it take to achieve this goal? Determine a dollar figure, then list the accounts or converted business it will take to achieve that figure. Determine how many units the team must sell, then break it out per rep.

Think strategically. Any manager can be a box checker: 3-day field visits, field visit letters, weekly call ins, bi-weekly conference calls. But are you thinking big? Are you setting goals to knock down big customers with your sales team and then laying out strategic plans to accomplish those goals and targets?

Every company sets a forecast on a region/division and on a territory basis. The forecast is usually what the average region and representative will need to sell in order for the company, the manager, and the representative to hit their forecasts. If you want to be region of the year, find out what last year's region of the year sold in order to win. Set your goal higher and break that number out for each rep. When individual goals are set, add a certain dollar amount to each for the stretch goals. Let the reps know the target for helping the team hit the stretch goal and win region of the year. It's easy to assign a number, but does each individual have the desire to help the team achieve the goal?

Go through this process for each goal you wish to achieve. Maybe you would like each team member to win an award trip. If three of your six people achieve that goal, then it may almost ensure that you win an award trip. Help your reps determine what they will need to do to win a trip. (It may not be their goal, so be sure that is a motivation. If it is, help them set the goal and the actions steps to win.)

Review everyone's progress toward the various goals at least on a monthly basis. Even better, review goals on a weekly basis. Most salespeople like recognition. People like to see and hear their name in lights. On your bi-weekly or monthly conference call, be sure to announce where everyone stands against forecast and rankings.

———◆———

Dean:

Having written, specific goals, communicated regularly to your team is one of the most important and powerful steps in achieving success for the team and for each person individually. I attribute that step in large part to what I have achieved in my career both as a manager and as a sales rep.

———◆———

Dave:

Have your direct reports set their goals. Discuss with each of your people. Once you have reviewed these goals, go ahead and set the team goals based on this input. Sales representative goals and your goals must be measurable. They should also be attainable with some stretch. Push yourself. Discuss these goals with your team and set the expectation. Constantly update each teammate and the entire team on progress.

31

UNDERSTAND AND HELP ACHIEVE YOUR SALESPEOPLE'S GOALS (LONG TERM AND SHORT TERM)

It is the nature of man to rise to greatness if greatness is expected of him.
- John Steinbeck, Author

DON'T JUST UNDERSTAND YOUR sales representatives' goals; help each person achieve those goals. Some of your reps will want to go into management. If they are great sale reps and do a good job, help develop them to become great managers. Give them advice and coaching. If they earn it, give them additional responsibilities on the team. Enroll them in courses. Encourage them to grow, to learn, and to take on more responsibility. Get them in management development training, and if your company doesn't have one create your own. Get them involved with interviewing new candidates. Have them lead conference calls. Let them do field visits with some of your struggling reps.

Maybe a rep doesn't want to be in sales management. He/she may want to go into marketing. Put the rep in touch with a marketing director to help mentor the sales rep along the way. As we pointed out before, don't be afraid of losing your top people to promotion. Encourage them and support them, and they will do an even better job for you if they know you are behind them.

Communicate with your reps and truly understand their goals. Review goals during each field visit.

Dean:

One major reason salespeople leave companies is that the position doesn't seem to mesh with individual goals anymore. They may want to be promoted, but they don't feel it will happen there. Be aware of goals and help achieve them.

---◆---

Dave:

When your top performers are asking for more responsibility, several things have to happen: 1) In your opinion, are they ready for more responsibility? 2) What if you don't think they are good enough to be a sales leader; what do you do? You tell them in a very empathic way. You owe it to them to be honest. 3) Finally, begin mapping out a strategy to help your superstars achieve their personal career goals. Once they see you begin to "sell" them to upper management, I guarantee you their performances will peak because they are saying "thank you for supporting me and in believing in me."

> *Goals are dreams with deadlines.*
> *- Diana Scharf Hunt, author*

32

KEEP YOUR MANAGER WELL-INFORMED ON ISSUES

*It isn't the people you fire who will make your life miserable,
it's the people you don't fire.*

- Harvey Mackay

AGAIN, WE AREN'T ENCOURAGING ANYONE to become an "ax man," but you will have poor-performing salespeople, and you will need to deal with them. One of the ways to protect yourself and motivate your people is to keep your VP or Director copied and apprised on the good, the bad, and the ugly when it comes to your salespeople. Make it a habit of copying your manager on a lot of the communication. If someone does well, give them recognition by copying the team and your manager.

IF SOMEONE DOES SOMETHING BAD, NEVER DISCIPLINE OR COMMUNICATE NEGATIVE THINGS ABOUT THE REP IN FRONT OF THE REST OF THE TEAM BUT CERTAINLY COPY YOUR MENTOR AND POTENTIALLY HR.

Some upper management people don't like to drag HR into things, but on some issues, you need to protect yourself by copying HR.

An HR director can make or break you as a manager. If he/she is weak, he will never try to understand the manager's point of view. He will always side with the rep because he may be afraid of a lawsuit. This rarely happens, but when it does, you will be in a very difficult situation. If you can't properly manage, coach, and sometimes discipline your reps without fear of backlash from the rep or HR, it is like trying to walk without a spine. Sure, HR is there to protect managers as well as employees. There are bad managers against whom reps must be protected, but an HR director or department must stand strong with the managers.

Unfortunately, in this litigious society, too many employees, including managers, make false claims against companies, managers, and others. The minute the heat is on and they are backed into a corner, they start trying to figure out ways to strike back. The best way to protect yourself and never have to worry about lawsuits or problems is: (these are important)

1) **Document everything through e-mails and field visit letters.**

2) If it is a serious issue, make sure HR is copied on the e-mails and letters.

3) Copy your manager and, if need be, the VP or director of sales.

4) Communicate verbally with your salespeople, then follow up in writing with a FVL.

5) Don't be a bad manager and do unethical things. Don't make sexual advances towards your reps; don't make off-color comments or, worse, racist, sexual, sexist or religious comments; don't play favorites; manage fairly; and use common sense.

6) Always do the right thing, even if it isn't the popular thing.

7) Keep your direct manager in the loop; don't give him/her any surprises.

———◆———

Dean:

No one likes paperwork, but you must document, and you must keep people informed if you want their support to take action on an employee. Remember, you owe it to your salespeople to give them feedback, whether good or bad.

———◆———

Dave:

Better safe than sorry. There is no way you can over document. Simply put, documenting issues, e-mails, conversations, etc., are all components in building a case for termination.

33

INSPIRE AND MOTIVATE YOUR TEAM AND EACH INDIVIDUAL

A leader has the vision and conviction that a dream can be achieved. He inspires the poser and energy to get it done.
- Ralph Lauren, fashion designer

THERE ARE SO MANY WAYS to motivate salespeople, both as individuals and as a team. Hopefully, everyone on your team has bought into the desire to win region/division of the year. If the award is called division manager of the year, refer to it as division of the year. If you win, have a celebration afterward, and award each rep with a division of the year plaque with all the team members' names.

Let your reps know at the beginning of the year that if the team wins the award you will have a **"division meeting" at some exotic location** (if the company will allow it). It doesn't have to be too expensive. If you live in Florida or California, do it at a beach resort. If you live in New York, go to Martha's Vineyard. Be creative. Call it a division meeting, and no one should give you a hard time. Meet in the morning and play in the afternoon. Invite spouses or significant others. The hotel rooms are already paid for, so spend an extra $1,000 to treat them to a nice dinner. The company will get the money back tenfold, and it will be a fantastic team-building experience for all involved. The spouses will get a better understanding of what their husbands and wives do and with whom you work, and it will be better for your people's personal lives as well. Nothing beats it and hopefully your company or VP will support it.

At the big dinner, present the division of the year plaques as well as some **individual awards for division/region performance**. You can have a division sales representative of the year award, greatest % growth award, largest dollar volume award, and the list goes on. They will be very proud to win these in front of their significant others, and it is all very motivating and rewarding. It will also further inspire new hires, just as the national sales meeting hopefully did. Word of caution: some companies will want to count any award over a certain dollar amount as income.

Give out a sales representative of the month award. Try to base it somewhat on the formula the company is using for sales representative of the year award, which will help ensure people are focusing on the right things. Some might think it is a little bush league, but most don't and are motivated to do well. Give away a nice certificate created on the computer and if possible, give a $200 gift certificate for the winner and $100 to the second-place finisher each month. Again, just make sure there are no problems with the company or any tax issues if you do this.

Verbally announce the division sales rankings both for the month and the year to date at the end of each month on a conference call. The people at the bottom won't like it, but they will work harder to get off the bottom. You have to weigh everything in management, however. There aren't any black-and-white rules. Some years, the people at the bottom may just not be pulling their weight, so maybe you announce the entire rankings at month's end. In some instances, though, the bottom person may be struggling due to no fault of his/her own. Maybe the rep is new, and prior to that person's arrival a rep may have left after loading up all the accounts to receive a last commission check. This may have left the territory struggling and announcing the last-place finish every month will be a de-motivator instead of a motivator. If it were you near the bottom, would you need to be reminded every month? Of course not! However, if someone is lazy and not giving his/her all, you might want to announce that rep's last-place finish.

Follow up your verbal announcement with a written summary of the rankings. Try to find some way to recognize everyone if you can, unless you have someone who really doesn't deserve any recognition. You've got to decide if you want to motivate a poor performer or if you'd rather he/she just leave the company. If you want to try to motivate the rep, find something positive to recognize in his/her work. If you'd rather the rep just leave, that decision will determine your strategy in constructing a performance plan. Copying your Director or VP can add a nice touch of recognition.

If you have a leader within your team, someone you may be grooming for advancement or someone who is highly respected, have him/her buddy up with a struggling rep. That's not to say you shouldn't be coaching or helping each member of your team, but sometimes reps respond nicely to a peer—a successful representative. You could easily set up a mentoring program.

Recognize and appreciate the efforts of ancillary people who help your team, such as customer service, shipping, HR, and R&D. Once a quarter or at least once a year, treat customer service to lunch. If you can't be there, have it delivered with your compliments. Make sure you go around, get to know, and visit all key people when visiting the home office. It's the right thing to do, and people tend to help those they know and like. Always treat them with respect, too!

———◆———

Dean:

The difference between great sales teams and poor- performing sales teams can often be linked to how well the manager brings out the best and motivates his/ her people. Remember what we've said though—don't expect to hire B and C level players and win any awards.

———◆———

Dave:

Communicate, communicate, communicate. Be a cheerleader. Selling is tough enough. Most of your team will respond much better to positive reinforcement. Be an encourager. Stand behind your representatives. Managing through intimidation went away with the typewriter. Join the rest of us who believe that encouragement goes a long way!

34

CREATE TEAMWORK

Team spirit is what gives so many companies an edge over their competition.

- George Clements

SET SOME COMMON GOALS FOR **the team** so that each person not only strives for his/her own individual goal, but also works together with the team. Hopefully, you have set the goal to be region of the year or division of the year. Some individuals don't get excited about this award and will try to diminish its importance among the team. The first question in trying to get the entire team invested in going after this award is, "What's in it for your team?" Earlier we talked about having a division meeting to celebrate with the spouses should your team win. Use that as a motivator for the team. Usually, if any of your people has played team sports, he/she is naturally motivated to win this type award. You may not win over those one or two people who just don't "get it." That type person is usually your low performer, not always, but usually. Who doesn't want to be on a team to win the National Championship? Non-athlete? Not competitive? Or could be a lone wolf. (see The Challenger Sale about Lone Wolves)

Another way to create teamwork is to **"buddy up" the more tenured reps with the newer reps.** In addition to the field sales trainer who may be assigned to your newer reps, you might consider assigning a mentor within the group. This could be a strong, tenured rep who doesn't want to be a field sales trainer. Two points here:

1) Hopefully, you have a strong enough field sales trainer within your team who can usually train your new salespeople. This builds natural teamwork.

2) If you have concerns about your FST training your people, maybe that person shouldn't be a field sales trainer. Always strive to have the best field sales trainers training your people. If you must go out of your division to ensure this, then do, but then again, you must question as to whether your FST is the right person in the job.

Have periodic division/region meetings, maybe twice a year or once a quarter. There are usually two national meetings a year for most companies so, combined with your two-four division meetings, that should be plenty. Take each time that you get together as a time to build teamwork. If you have two National Meetings which allow for division/region time, no need to have six meetings. Just two-four total should suffice. If the company doesn't have a team or region dinner night, then you should plan to have one. During your division/region meetings, make sure you leave time to do something fun that will build teamwork. Don't make the meetings over two days; usually a day and a half plus a team building event at night is good.

———◆———

Dean:

If you ever expect to win division manager of the year, you must get your salespeople working together as a team while at the same time creating some fun, non-threatening competition within the group as well. All the low-performing teams I took over, the sales people were working independently of each other. Like a great football team, you'll never win a championship unless everyone is working together as a team, which is something I begin working on from day one.

One touch challenge I had was when one tenured, successful rep wanted to control the other sales reps, and when I came into the company, he tried to turn the team against me. So, I quickly isolated him, bringing upper management up to speed and informing them as to what was going on. I let them know that in order to turn the group into a winning team I needed management support, which they gave me. In this sort of situation, when you have a tenured rep trying to tear apart the team, it is very difficult to get anything done if upper management allows a successful rep to hold the company hostage. They've got to allow you to manage for the good of the team and the company as a whole. In this case, upper management did a beautiful job in supporting me. I was able to create the team environment I needed, and in year two we came in Runner-Up Region of the Year; only second due to a bulk order placed on December 31 by the winning team at an unheard-of price. Then in year three we won region of the year. I could not have done it without a strong director of sales and HR director supporting me. The tenured rep got in line and helped the team both years, but without the support from my VP and HR, I don't think we would have done as well as a team.

———◆———

Dave:

One time to create teamwork is during sales promotions. I would always ask, "Who wants to lead this promotion for our division/region?" Most of the time, the person I wanted to lead was the one who was not doing very well selling a particular focus, brand product. This would force that individual to learn and sell more in order to maintain credibility. Peer pressure is a wonderful motivator. Let me say that one more time: Peer pressure is a wonderful motivator.

We set our team expectations high. Coming in second place in a national promotion was not acceptable, period, end of sentence! I wanted our team to strive to be the best. Once we began winning everything, the winning attitude carried over into everything we did as a team. We felt good about ourselves. Sales professionals were being compensated for excelling and being recognized as the top division! It quickly became habit-forming and expected.

35

EMPOWER YOUR PEOPLE TO BE SOLUTIONS-ORIENTED

It is impossible to get the measure of what an individual can accomplish, unless the responsibility is placed on him. - Alfred Sloan,

General Motors chairman

THE WORST THING A MANAGER can do is to come up with all the ideas and all the solutions. Make sure when one of your salespeople comes to you with a problem or opportunity, you ask the person to give you two or three options to attack it. This will make him/her a better business person, and it will make the rep accountable for his/her success or failure. If you make the decisions or come up with the ideas and tactics all the time, when the ideas fail, who is to blame? Be sure you strongly encourage your people to think creatively, and never belittle an idea.

Everyone believes they have all the answers and solutions. Ideas, trends, solutions, strategies float up from the field, and so often they are shut down. No one listens. Then, when the trend becomes a problem, the original idea is later incorporated, often too late. Listen to your sales people and be there voice to the company. Not every idea can be accepted; not all are good. Flush them out with the reps.

Dean:

Not only is it important to get your people to be solutions-oriented, but most salespeople don't like micromanagers. Always coming up with all the answers is one form of micromanagement. Rick Puleo, my manager in my second year of medical sales said to me, "Dean, come to me with some suggestions and solutions to solve your problems. We'll talk about them, brainstorm, bounce them around, and together we'll decide, but don't come to me with just the problem." He was helping me develop into a manager, and I'll never forget those words. That was the best thing he could have ever done for me.

Empower your people!

<hr>

Dave:

This is so true! How many times have your sales professionals come to you with problems? Every day? If that's the case, it's not their fault; it's yours for not teaching them to bring a solution along with an idea or problem. After the problem has been discussed, consider several courses of action, and, ultimately, let the sales professional make the final decision! Empower them. Encourage them. Soon, they won't be coming to you nearly as much. Guaranteed!

<hr>

Don't micromanage.

The fastest way to lose your team is to be on their backs about everything. Teach them to think for themselves. If they have issues, ask them to come to you with solutions.

<hr>

Dave:

Empowering your team begins the day you hire each person. Set the tone immediately. Let your new hires know that you are there to help them. No question is a dumb question. Encourage. Little wins begin to build confidence. Confidence builds on itself. Support them if they make mistakes. However, continue to empower. How else will you be able to effectively build up someone if the person doesn't think you believe in him/her?

> *There is no value judgment more important to man; no factor more decisive in his psychological development and motivation than the estimate he passes on himself.*
> *- Nathaniel Branden, author and philosopher*

36

GET YOUR PEOPLE INVOLVED IN SALES MEETINGS

An organization's ability to learn, and translate that learning into action rapidly, is the ultimate competitive, business advantage.
- Jack Welch, former General Electric CEO

NO ONE LIKES TO HEAR his/her managers get up and pontificate and philosophize for two or three days at a meeting. Make the meeting your representatives' meeting. In addition to the things you will need to cover, find out what issues are important to your reps. What issues would they like to discuss? Send out a voicemail and ask. If they don't come back with anything, then pick the things you believe are important, lay out the agenda, and then ask them to prepare for discussion of each topic. You might have individuals conduct the discussion or have teams of two. Make the meeting an opportunity for everyone to learn from each other and from that will come ideas and solutions that may just help the company.

At the meeting, encourage open discussion. Get people talking about their successes, problems, and failures. You will find that people learn more when they are involved in the process, rather than you just standing up there with 200 slides that put them to sleep.

———◆———

Dean:

The best way to get people really involved in a meeting, to really walk away with some valuable information, is to have them prepare for the meeting and help you conduct it. When you get people involved, they stay awake and they learn. I've done this throughout my career, and it works like a charm. How many meetings have you attended where the speaker puts up 100 slides, everyone falls asleep, and people later say the meeting was a waste of time? I'm guessing a lot. So don't do it.

In addition, schedule the meetings in productive hours and hold to it. While OR reps are used to being up at 5 a.m., 6 a.m. to get to surgery, when it comes to learning, hold the meetings from 9-5. People plan a day and a half meeting and then they try to cram two days' worth of information in. In addition, other departments ask to come, and they end up cramming even more into the meeting. No one learns after 5 p.m. I had an Area Director who used to stick his five managers in a room with no windows then stand up and talk for almost the entire day. He started at 8 a.m. and would hold us until 6 or 6:30 p.m. We all stopped listening to him around 2 p.m. and were crawling out of our skins by 4 p.m.   Can you imagine?   We actually learned a few things in the morning, but no one can listen to the same person for nine or ten hours.

———◆———

Dave:

What a super way to get your next generation of leaders involved. Put those on your team who are struggling with selling a particular product in charge of leading the discussion. This will force teammates to spend time learning more about this product they are struggling to sell. Hopefully, with input from others during the meeting, your struggling representative will begin to sell. Encourage. Coach them up!! After all, as a sales leader, you are a coach.

37

HOW TO HELP YOUR NEW SALESPEOPLE

The proof that you know something is that you are able to teach it.

- Aristotle, philosopher

YOU HOPEFULLY WERE PROMOTED OR hired into management because you demonstrated leadership qualities, an expertise in your industry, and an ability to teach. Whether you like it or not, part of sales management is developing your people and teaching. Your new salespeople are depending on you to ensure they get the proper training that will allow them to succeed. If you are a new manager with a company with no prior knowledge of the products, you need to ensure that if you can't initially be involved with their education because you are too new with the company, you can find people who can teach them. In the meantime, you need to get enough working knowledge of the products that you can: 1) effectively help train new reps in the future, 2) have intelligent conversations with customers on the products with your salespeople, and 3) effectively handle sales calls on your own if need be. You are going to need to be able to help your new and tenured salespeople learn new sales techniques or ways to attack their business; so you better get up to speed quick.

Immediately, upon your new hire being onboard, **you need to make sure that "pre-learning material" arrives at their homes** so they can begin learning asap. You might assign pre-work, prior to their first day, or have sales training assign pre-learning that doesn't divulge proprietary information. Of course, you'll need to make sure they passed a background check, etc., before you have pre-training material shipped out that does include confidential information. Remember though, rarely is learning material automatically shipped. Call sales training or the marketing department to make sure the training material is sent.

When is the next training class? Sometimes it is not for a month or two after hiring an individual. You'll need to **meet with your new sales rep** and you should conduct a training program with him/her if a training class is too far off in the future. If not you, then get a field sales trainer in there to get them up to speed.

Every company is different on when they will allow a new hire can hit the field. Some companies want a rep to have completed 100% of all new hire training before they will allow them to interact with a customer; period. You certainly don't want a new hire to go out there ill prepared, lose sales, etc.

It really depends on how complicated your products are and what type of products you sell. You've got to be careful. The bottom line is you want to get that new hire properly trained as fast as possible and in the field. Again, if you are a new manager, get your new rep with an experienced employee. This could be a marketing product manager or a field sales trainer. Also, if you are new, always go through training as well. Don't be afraid that you'll look bad. You need to be trained and you need to become an expert. We've seen too many managers who know nothing about the products and their respects find them useless. How can you teach if you don't know anything about the products? Hoping you learn on the job is not a strategy. At a minimum, go spend a few days or a week with a field sales trainer outside your division/region.

You could also **have a new hire do a fellowship** with a customer, serving two purposes. First, customers usually love training new people, especially if you pay them for it. Second, it allows the sales rep to build a strong relationship with one of your more important customers.

Whatever you do, you must **make sure your salesperson has the proper training** to succeed, from the standpoint of helping your team but also from a legal and HR standpoint. If you do not ensure this and a rep fails, the person can come back at the company for letting him/her go and claim he/she didn't have the proper training everyone else had. It is very important that the company have a standard program for training that everyone receives. It doesn't necessarily have to happen inside a training room, but if the standard is that every new salesperson spends three weeks in the home office and two weeks in the field with a field sales trainer, then you'd better make sure that your new sales reps spend three weeks in the home office and two with a FST, regardless of whether the FST is first and the home office second or vice versa. Any additional training you do yourself is merely further assurance that the rep will have the tools necessary to succeed.

While a new hire is in training, don't allow the rep's territory to fall apart and slip in sales. Pay attention. Make sure either you or another salesperson is checking a contact for customers and answering calls and requests. You've got to also spend a few hours calling customers and letting them know whom to call or to call you. It is easy to just hope for the best or ignore someone else's messages, but in the long run, it is only going to hurt you. You may take the attitude of "whatever happens during training happens, and we'll worry about it all when training is over," but that's dangerous for business. When you hired that person, he/she was told the amount of money that could be earned by hitting quota or "plan." What you didn't say was that the person was going to be in training for two months and during that time you were going to allow the territory to slip in sales so much the rep's first-year income would be affected.

Consider assigning another salesperson to cover the new hire's territory, and make sure compensation is given for the extra work. This, however, may not the best approach. Try to cover it yourself, if you can, because one of your other sales reps may be too focused on their own territory. Another approach would be to have someone from the home office cover the territory. There may be a customer service rep who would like to get out in the field. There may be a product manager who would like to carry the bag for a few weeks to get a better understanding of the business. Just make sure that no matter who you have covering is not going to make matters worse.

Get out in the field with your new sales rep early on, not to micromanage but to give a "leg-up" and help him/her jump out of the gate strong. You can let the rep spend a week or two on his/her own getting around meeting new customers, but plan to spend three days with the rep within the first month.

If you know the territory well because it was previously your territory, consider riding with the rep the first week to make it easier for him/her to meet new customers.

Ensure the former rep leaves a detailed accounting of the territory, what is going on in each account, the key customers and contact lists, and any other pertinent information that's needed. If the former salesperson was promoted within the company, make sure beforehand that all agree the former rep will be allowed to spend a week in the territory with the new rep introducing him/her to customers.

If the former rep was good but is leaving the company, make sure he/she leaves the information. If you can trust the person, try to get him/her to come back and spend a week as a favor to you. Make sure the reason the rep left will not be a distraction or discouragement to your new person. If the old rep is leaving because he/she was frustrated with the company, its comp plan, etc., then **you don't want him/her to meet the new sales rep.**

38

LET YOUR COLTS RUN, BUT KEEP A REIN ON THEM

You got to have rules, but you also gotta allow for a fella to mess up once in a while.

- Coach Bum Phillips

SOME OF YOUR BEST SALESPEOPLE are going to be a little rough around edges. They might be vocal at meetings, raising eyebrows with upper management. They may be very aggressive, irritating a few customers, but the bottom line is they are excellent salespeople.

Some managers will want to put a "razor wire bit" on them and jerk them back. (Excuse the horse training jargon.) They'll want to beat them down into submission and try to take the spirit out of them. Other managers won't know how to manage them; thus, they'll just let them buck and kick, irritating upper management and customers to the point of risking their jobs.

Great managers will know how to pull the reins back and as they say, "Keep a tight rein on them" without taking the life out of them. If you take either of the first two approaches: 1) They will become unhappy because they aren't going to want to take the beating. 2) Upper management will think they "don't fit the image" of the company and will want them out.

You've got to stand up for these type salespeople and let them know you are behind them 100%, that you appreciate their abilities, and that you will go to bat for them when they need things. **However**, if they want your support, and they want you to go to bat for them, they need to work with you. They need to be open to taking feedback and training. They need to avoid embarrassing you as a manager because if they do that, they need to understand that they will lose your support. As long as you lay it out for them, and you get agreement that you are on the same team, you should have a long-lasting, productive relationship. It can work, but you've got to be ready to discipline them when they get out of line.

---◆---

Dean:

Learn how to bridle that enthusiasm and aggression of a salesperson, and you'll have some of the best salespeople you'll ever manage. Be afraid, work against them, or just give up and get rid of them, and you will have made a horrible mistake in your career.

Take a great, spirited sales rep who is a little rough around the edges, beat that person up with disparaging comments, and not only will you make him/her a nervous wreck when in front of your customers, but the rep also may never live up to his/her potential.

One of the great expressions I heard early on as a manager is: I'd rather have to pull the reins back on a thoroughbred then to have to beat a mule.

39

BE STRONG AND BE TOUGH WHEN YOU HAVE TO

To see what is right and not do it is a lack of courage.
                                                - Confucius, philosopher

THERE WILL BE TIMES WHEN you'll have to be tough and you'll have to have courage. If you think it is easy to fire someone, then: 1) You have no compassion for people. Or, 2) You've never done it.

But, as a manager, the company pays you to handle the good and the bad. Sometimes, no matter what you do to help someone, he/she just doesn't respond, or the job just isn't a good fit. In sales, if you take the customer through the entire sales process, the close won't be quite as tough. Skip some of the steps in between, and the close will not only be a lot more difficult, your chance of getting the sale will be a lot lower. Same with coaching and developing. As we discussed earlier: spring surprises on people and your task of letting someone go becomes that much harder. Give them honest oral and written feedback and it becomes a lot less complicated.

If you have a difficult or non-performing employee and you have done a good job of documenting and informing the rep of his/her lackluster performance, then it should not come as any surprise when you finally let the person go. Skip all the steps in between, and you may have an argument and tough situation on your hands.

If you avoid getting rid of your weak, low performing sales reps, you will not only be letting the company down, but you'll be letting down customers, stockholders and yourself. In addition, you be letting down the sales representative as well.

Many times, it takes a good kick in the rear end to get someone serious about life and his/her job. Sometimes those below-average salespeople, after leaving your company, will finally get the message that life is not a dress rehearsal. They may go on to incredible careers, and had you allowed them to continue limping along, their performance would probably never improve and very possibly would continue to decline.

So, here are the steps to helping or eventually firing a poor performer:

1) **Give verbal feedback during field visits and follow it up with the field visit letter.** Summarize performance and why it is unacceptable. Suggest one or two major things to improve performance. Be sure to copy your manager on the letters.

2) **Follow up field visit letters on your weekly calls.** Don't wait until the next field visit, which could be 6-12 weeks away, to check in on progress, brainstorm, and come up with alternate strategies if things are progressing with the sales targets.

3) **Have open discussion and raise the bar on the next field visit letter**. If a poor performer is not improving and not taking steps to improve, then you need to re-emphasize the unacceptable performance and behavior and use words like, "I am concerned," and "Your current sales performance is unacceptable." Remember, you must be verbally communicating this during your field visit. If you are merely sending it in an e-mail or field visit letter, you are taking the wrong, easy way out.

4) **Next step prior to a formalized performance plan may be a warning letter**. Some companies may allow you to go straight to a performance plan but again, you should want to give your people the opportunity to turn it around, but if it is obvious they are in the wrong position, you may go straight to the performance plan.

Now, if you are seeing improvement and the rep is really trying, you should commend him/her and recognize the effort. Realize that this isn't the norm. Most poor performers do not all of a sudden turn their lives around, but every once in a while, you may motivate someone to change. But if you give them a warning letter and they respond, then you can either keep them on a type of probationary period or pull back and take them off the warning. But, again, unfortunately, the improvement is often temporary, and you will have to move forward to place them on a formalized performance plan.

5) **Put the rep on a formalized performance plan**. Don't feel like you have failed because a below-average person does not become an all-star under your mentorship. People don't usually change a lifetime of attitude, but it is possible. Be an optimist and believe you can have a positive impact on someone's life and sales ability. Just don't be down on yourself if you can't save someone from losing his/her job. You can feel bad about having to let anyone go, but just don't blame yourself because they wouldn't take the steps to succeed. As we said, sometimes it's the kick in the pants he/she needs to make a change.

If you don't see improvement by the second or third field visit (and the field visits should be increasing in frequency at this point), then you will need to put the poorly performing representative on a formalized performance plan. Based on the prior performance and how long this has been going on, you may need to move quickly on that person. But remember, as a new manager, you must balance the effect it may have on the entire team. If the team views you as being unfair or a hatchet man/woman right out of the gate, it could be detrimental to the team overall. This is where the art of leadership comes in. Some people may say, "You can't wait to move on replacing a poor performing sales person." Yes, in most cases, this is true but as a new manager, you've got to establish some trust and credibility with the team.

Depending on the poor performer's attitude and the policy of the company, determine if the rep should go on a 30-, 60-, or 90-day plan. If someone is belligerent and argumentative at this point, you may just want to get rid of him/her in 30 days. If you've been documenting performance all along, this may be possible. If you truly feel the rep wants to change or wants to try, you can make the plan 60 or 90 days. If his/her attitude is more that of acceptance and understanding, but you both know that he/she can't do the job, you may give the employee 60 days. However, if you believe in your heart through your discussion that the rep truly wants to change and will take your guidance and direction, give him/her 90 days to turn it around.

———◆———

Dean:

Very few people I put on performance plans worked themselves off a performance plan. The objectives were obtainable, but the rep didn't have the natural drive and determination to "get it done." In some instances, the people just left before their performance plan periods ran out. They knew the gig was up. In other instances, I had to let them go. Some rare times, those which were the most rewarding, the reps not only worked themselves off the plan but went on to win awards and become top salespeople. For me, those were some of the most memorable, rewarding accomplishments as a manager.

A few success stories come to mind. One guy I really liked as a person, just wasn't a driven salesperson. His work ethic was below average, and he never lived up to his potential. It really bothered me to put him on a plan, but I knew I had to do it. Well, he did work off the plan and never looked back. He went on to win awards and glamour award trips and eventually went into management.

Another guy was very difficult to manage. Everyone else was to blame for his problems, in his mind. He was one I probably hoped would just leave during the plan. But he also managed to work himself off the plan. It seemed as though he matured. He began taking responsibility and became accountable for his successes and failures. After I left the company, he eventually become a manager for another company. Most other instances in which I had to put people on plans did not have such positive outcomes.

———◆———

Dave:

When I put someone on a plan, he/she was gone in my mind. I just had to go through the mental gymnastics with HR, etc., to cover myself. However, it took A LOT for me to decide this was the end of the road. With some, I was probably too patient. However, more times than not, that patience paid off.

Selling is about producing. When a rep knows he/she is not getting it done over the course of time, a decision needs to be made. Usually I would ask a person in trouble if the person felt he/she could make it. The answer was always "yes." Again, I had to make the decision if **I** felt the rep could make it. If so, I would support the heck out of him/her. If not, the rep was on a plan.

As a manager, if you do everything you can to develop people, understand what is going on in their lives, and give them the chance to turn it around, you can never feel guilty if THEY choose not to try, not to work hard, not to take your guidance and direction.

40

BE A LEADER, NOT JUST A MANAGER

People grow through experience if they meet life honestly and courageously. This is how character is built.
- Eleanor Roosevelt, first lady

YOUR PEOPLE WILL LOOK TO you for leadership. No matter what company you work for, tough times will come. You can work for the greatest company in the world, but eventually there will be major backorders, no new products in the pipeline, recalls, competitors, and big price increases that put business at risk. There will be something that causes your people to panic. An oldie but goodie: "When the going gets tough, the tough get going?" There's another saying: "When the going gets tough, the weak get going ... out the door."

Did you ever wonder why some divisions have high turnover while others have a lot less? We're talking about unwanted turnover. Part of it is due to leadership. As a leader, you've got to give people hope. You've got to keep them informed. You've got to lay out the facts. You've got to put things in perspective. You've got to prevent turnover from getting out of control during tough times. Even when the weak reps leave, it can cause a domino effect during difficult periods. You must get the strong reps "on board" and "bought into" the future. Massive turnover can be the death of a sales team. If you lose a weak link or two, it won't be the end of the world, but you MUST keep turnover under control.

If you are a strong leader and a great mentor, people will hang in there longer. If you are a strong leader, many people would rather fight with you than go to an unknown manager. If you are a weak leader and your people believe the ship is sinking, they'll be the first to jump into the life boats. If you've built a strong team environment, they trust and respect you, and if you provide a plan for all of them to weather the storm, they are more likely to stick around.

Those managers who just become silent, mislead their teams, and do nothing usually suffer the worst. It happens time and time again. During tough times, weak leaders lose 50-75% of their teams, whereas strong leaders may lose 5-20%.

Unless you work for a startup, very few established companies go under. You've got to be the captain of the ship. If things are that bad, you may leave too, but if you are willing to stay, then you need to help the team "batten down the hatches" and ride the storm. Help them understand what we just said, "No matter where they go, there will eventually be tough times." If they keep bouncing every time the water gets rough, eventually their resumes will become that of "bouncers" and getting a job with a great company will get tougher and tougher.

To be great manager, you need to be and usually is a great leader. A manager is someone who tactically checks the boxes. A leader is someone who people will follow into a battle. A king is not a king unless he has people who will follow him.

> *Do what is right, not what you think the high headquarters wants or what you think will make you look good.*
> *- Norman Schwarzkopf, general*

Have you ever heard of a "brown-noser"? Not a good visual, but you know what it means. Did you ever like a brown-noser? Did you ever respect a brown-noser? Do you think your salespeople or anyone else in your company will respect you, including upper management if you are a brown-noser? Then DON'T BE ONE.

Companies are looking for leaders. They are looking for people who will have the guts to lead, to offer up ideas, and who will help keep the company on track. They aren't looking for yes men/women. That's often the reason why they must hire consultants, because managers don't have the guts to tactfully, positively discuss the challenges they face and the solutions to fix them. If you ever see a sales team in which the managers are afraid to speak up in leadership meetings, tactfully, during tough time, usually big changes are on the horizon—middle management will have a big shakeup to try and fix the problems, upper management will eventually have a change because the board determines they are the problems, there will be a massive layoff, there will be a massive move to purge underperforming sales people, comp plans will be overhauled to incredibly reward performing reps and severely penalize underperforming reps, or eventually the division/company will fail. Those managers who survive are usually those who continue to come forward with solutions and who lead; not those who agree with the captain of a ship with a big hole in the hull that they probably just hit some rough water; but no biggee; full steam ahead.

> *Opportunity is missed by most people because it is dressed in overalls and looks like work.*
> *- Thomas Edison, inventor*

Another way to lead by example is to work hard. If you sit in your office every week and never get out to work with your reps, if you refuse to cover for your reps when they go on vacation or are sick, or if you are never available when your reps call for assistance, then you are setting a horrible example to your team and will be an average manager at best. Hard work can overcome a lot of obstacles in a year. The company may be having hard times, your products may be outdated, competition may be on the rise, but if you work hard, you will stay on top of the rankings and on top of the competition. Never minimize the importance of hard work and the example you set for the rest of your team.

And let us stress it again; teach your reps to be challengers, to change paradigms, and to bring more value to the table then just your outdated products. If you can get your reps to present themselves as partners with the customers, as consultants, and as advisors who can help enhance and understand the customer's business by insuring your products are part of those paradigm shifts, this will help overcome a lot of deficiencies in the company or in your product line. It is through this way of doing business today which develops deeper relationships. It's not about who took the customer to the best dinner, but rather who can bring the most value to their business or practice. Products are a part of that mix, but we can do so much more for our customers if we just think out of the box and think strategically.

Dean:

Having been a manager and a recruiter, it is clear that one of the major reasons people look for new jobs is due to what they perceive as an unreasonable, horrible manager. It's usually the number one reason people are looking.

———◆———

Dave:

Leadership is the most important trait of an effective manager. Your team is looking for someone to follow. Will you be that person or just be their friend? Will you be the manager who is constantly micromanaging? Let me warn you. If you are a micromanager . . . you will come to hate your job. Great leaders learn to delegate. Micromanagers generally do not have the confidence to let go of the reins to allow their teams to run. Be a leader. Get out of the way. Give clear direction, inspect what you expect, and watch the confidence of you team grow. Also, their belief in you will grow. Lead!

41

STAND FIRM TO WHAT YOU BELIEVE

A leader, once convinced a particular course of action is the right one, must have the determination to stick with it and be undaunted when the going gets rough.
                    - Ronald Reagan, 40th U.S. president

TO BE A GREAT MANAGER, a great leader, a great human being, you've got to stand for what you believe to be the right thing ethically and morally, for the customer, for the company, for your sales team, and for yourself. Your team will lose respect for you, and you will lose respect for yourself if you do less. Often however, what's best for the company isn't always the best thing for your sales team. That's a tough place to be, but you got to lead through it.

Hopefully, the company will do the right thing and your people will understand that sometimes for the overall good of an organization, changes are made to save jobs and to ultimately save customers. Hopefully, your team has a sense for what you believe and overall that sense is that you stand for what is right, for what is fair, and for what is best—even if that doesn't always align with what they want. If you then compromise those beliefs, you lose the respect of your team and yourself.

As an example, your company may have allowed something in the past, such as free goods, etc., but maybe the laws have changed. The customer still hasn't gotten the memo and is still demanding free product and if you don't provide them, there is a big chance you might lose the business because that free product was effectively lowering their price. Nine out of ten times, you will not lose the business, but customers can be tough, but in the rep's mind, they are panicking.

You could quietly and secretly find a way to get the free product into the hands of the customer, but if caught, it could jeopardize the customer, the rep's job, your job, and the company could be fined heavily or even have a product shut down temporarily. You've got to lead the rep through this predicament. You've got to try and come up with other solutions, but ultimately you must do the right thing even if it means losing some business.

If the company wants you to fire someone who doesn't deserve to be fired, you've got to stand firm. If the company wants you to do something unethical, you've got to stand firm. If a customer asks you to do something unreasonable and unprofitable, you've got to stand firm. When representatives pressure you to do things for them that aren't fair to the others, you've got to stand firm.

Your heart or gut will normally tell you the right thing to do in every situation. If you aren't sure, ask a mentor or friend. Get some opinions. Reconfirm what you know to be true and then stand by your decision.

That doesn't mean if new facts are presented you have to be stubborn and inflexible. We're just saying that there will come times as a leader in which you will have to make tough decisions. You will have to stand up for what is right. You will have to stand up for your team, stand up for the customers, or stand up for the company. Do the right thing always, and you can reflect on your life and career and feel good about the path you chose.

Dean:

Great companies are looking for leaders—not yes-men/women. I have watched many yes-men let the door hit 'em from behind where the sun don't shine. They just didn't get it. When your team senses you are only out for yourself, you will lose their respect and your effectiveness. Make strong decisions, do what is right, let your inner moral compass lead you, and you will be a great manager. It's a balance, though. Like constantly complaining salespeople, managers who are whiney and negative are not viewed as leaders. Stay positive and come to the table with solutions.

Dave:

Do you want to be known as the guy/gal who drinks too much at every meeting and starts developing a reputation? Your team is watching you. As their leader, set the example. Know your belief system. Do not compromise. Your integrity is on the line every day.

> *It has been my philosophy of life that difficulties vanish when faced boldly.*
>
> *- Isaac Asimov, author*

42

You've Got to Be Fair

I try to do the right thing at the right time. They may just be little things, but usually they make the difference between winning and losing.
- Kareem Abdul-Jabbar, one of the greatest basketball players of all-time

NO MATTER WHAT COMPANY YOU work for, territories will eventually be split, rearranged, cut, moved, or removed. You name it. Most people don't like change. As a manager, embrace change and lead people through it. Whenever change occurs, reps panic, become angry, and may want to quit. The first thing you have to do is ensure you are properly explaining the new compensation plan to everyone. Most companies want people to be able to make the same amount of money each year provided there is deeper penetration and better coverage. New comp plans come along every year, so you've got to be good at figuring them out, creating examples, and explaining the plans to your sales people and how they can grow their incomes.

The minute companies change territories, add reps, and change comp plans, everyone yanks out their calculator, always sure they are going to get slammed. It is your job, as the leader, to carefully go through the comp plan with each rep individually.

Sometimes it will be your responsibility as the manager to realign the territories. So many companies today hire consulting companies to come in and realign based on statistics, but often they make mistakes in a few territories. Often, you'll get a chance to massage or tweak what the software has created. Reps are going to come lobbying to you for all the best accounts. It's OK, it's natural, and there's nothing wrong with getting input as to what reps would like to have. Just let them know that you MUST be fair to everyone and you must be fair to the new people to ensure they can earn a living, too. This is combining the art and science of leadership. If you penalize your tenured, great reps, they may leave if they will take a significant hit in income. If you don't provide new, potential all-stars with the ability to earn what you told them they could earn "at plan" with no "meat on the bone," they too may leave. You know your region, you should know your accounts, you should know the things a computer might not know. Speak up, be fair and do what is right for the team and the company overall.

What can happen and what often happens is upper management announces a new comp plan and states that "hitting plan" will result in everyone earning basically the same amount of income. But some managers will just give all the great accounts to the representatives already established. Then they go out and recruit people saying, "You can earn X amount at plan." The trouble with their "plan" is that most of their accounts are dog accounts, and their territory will never hit plan.

Sometimes managers will have two new territories, side by side, and give one of the two new reps a better territory intentionally. It could be a bad move. If you want long-term loyalty and long-term respect from your team, you must be fair to everyone. Yes, you may allow input from your best reps and even let them keep some of their favorite accounts, but you must give everyone an opportunity to earn a living and to keep their job. The worst thing you can do is hire someone into a "no-win situation." The rep could be devastated by the realignment and look bad when he/she is unable to achieve goal. Upper management is depending on you to understand the territories, to understand the logistics and the geography, and to map out equitable territories for everyone. When one of your reps finishes at 60% plan, he/she looks bad, but if your unfair splitting of territories clearly contributed to the failure, so do you.

What people often do is try to fix things in the short term, only to create nightmares for themselves in the long term. Be a leader and stand up for what is right. Sometimes you'll have to stand up to your best people and say, "I will do the best I can to give you some of the things you want, but understand it is my responsibility to ensure everyone can make a living within this division. The company has decided to add territories, so everyone will have to lose a few accounts they don't want to lose." In a managerial position, you can only do the best you can. If the company makes decisions on expansion or redirection, at least you can live with the fact that you did the best you could in a tough situation. You've got to think about your entire team, not just a few favorite reps. In order to win awards and be successful, you've got to get all your territories "humming" and producing. If you make bad decisions, you will have constant turnover, and that can spell disaster for you.

43

TROUBLEMAKERS AND NEGATIVE PEOPLE

The danger is not in the fall, but in failing to rise

- Anonymous

Troublemakers

YOU WILL PROBABLY RUN INTO some difficult employees who will challenge your patience. How you rise to the occasion and react to a problem will determine your effectiveness. We won't spend too much time on this because we would rather focus on the positive. Just know that if you manage long enough, you will run into those who are really out for themselves and are willing to do whatever it takes to whomever necessary to get ahead in this world. You will be challenged. Your integrity will be challenged, but if you always do the right things, take the high road, and are a strong, moral, and ethical leader, you will prevail. You may not prevail in that particular job or with that particular company, but everything happens for a reason. If you find yourself in a tough spot, not understanding why it seems as though bad people seem to be prevailing, know that you will be OK. In the end, maintain your moral and ethical compass, you will end up in a better place. Those who chose the wrong paths will get what they deserve eventually.

Unfortunately, troublemakers are sometimes good salespeople. Companies are hesitant to let this type of person go because the negative impact on other salespeople and on the company is not as apparent. The company and managers allow themselves to be held hostage by a troublemaker instead of doing what is necessary to make the whole team successful. Toxic people are just not worth the effort in an organization.

The point is that you always need to keep your eyes open to those around you. As we've said in other chapters, do what you need to do to protect yourself.

DOCUMENT EVERYTHING. There are a lot of good people out there. Don't be naïve, however, and let your guard down so that those who would take advantage of you or others can find the weakness in your armor.

———◆———

Dean:

I once had an average sales rep who worked for me whom everyone on the team disliked. He didn't get along with anyone; in fact, he irritated everyone, and he was out for himself. I decided to work with him, coach and develop him. I managed to salvage his job, and his performance went from average to above average. Then, unbeknownst to me, he decided he wanted my job. Not only did I mentor him on the social graces of working in a corporate environment and how to get along with people, but also, I mentored him on becoming a manager. Because the management program required relocation, and he didn't want to leave Los Angeles, he decided he wanted my job and went to incredible lengths to get it. He went to HR to complain about me. He lied and told HR that the rest of the team felt the same way.

He then quickly tried to get others to join his cause, bringing up false accusations. It was surreal, like something out of a movie. Thankfully, my team rallied behind me except for one person I had on a performance plan and this guy. During the few weeks this was going on, it was amazing. The HR director called a surprise meeting at our national sales meeting and didn't invite me. He brought all the reps into a room and allowed this guy the floor. Somehow in his twisted mind, he thought people would either remain quiet or would join the cause. Immediately, the rest of my team jumped to my defense, and, one by one, they laid into this guy. They publicly told the HR director and the director of sales what a fine manager I was and that this guy in NO way represented them. The issue went away, and this person looked very foolish. The director of sales was fired, and the HR director was moved to another role. Eventually, this guy left the company as well.

The moral of the story is that when you are successful, people will be jealous, and some will go as far as this rep was willing to go. If you manage long enough, you will encounter some bizarre situations. But if you always do the right thing, you document everything, and you treat people fairly, you will be ok.

When you have people on performance plans, some will do anything, whether it is moral or not, to protect themselves. How do you protect yourself? Once again for good measure: Be a good manager, treat people fairly, and document everything. Remember that HR is a vital partner and should be effective in helping you manage effectively while at the same time protecting sales people from incompetent or unfair managers. Keep HR informed along the way. The good news is that while I had this one bad experience with HR in my career, I have been fortunate to work with some of the finest HR directors in the industry who effectively helped me manage through other issues.

Ken Koharki at CORDIS Endovascular and Rose Ramon at CarboMedics are two who come to mind. They are the best of the best and played a large part in my success at both companies. Finally, it is still true that the good guy/gal will win in the end. You may face short-term setbacks and challenges, but through them, if you are living well, you will come out a stronger person and a stronger manager.

Be strong, stand by your conviction, and you will do fine.

—◆—

The man who complains about the way the ball bounces is likely to be the one who dropped it.
*   - Lou Holtz / college football coach*

Negative people

Negative people are never happy about anything—the compensation plan, their territories, the products they sell, the customers, their teammates, YOU, the director of sales . . . their lives. Every company has a grapevine of rumors, and usually it is rooted and grows in negative employees. They are the ones who instigate problems. They are like a cancer that spreads and may need to be removed. You need to help such people resolve their negativity quickly or help them find a new place where they might be happy. The sad thing is that negativity is a part of their lives and makeup. They are unhappy no matter where they go.

There is a difference between overreacting to negativity, becoming an ax-man, and giving people the benefit of the doubt. Sure, you must coach a rep, but if he/she continues to be a negative force, then you must take the necessary steps to correct a bad situation. Don't start cleaning house on your entire team because it could be years before you recover, but at the same time, don't be held hostage. You must inform the troublemaker that his/her behavior won't be tolerated. You must document the problems, and you must keep your mentor and human resources in the loop.

44

KNOW WHEN TO HOLD 'EM; KNOW WHEN TO FOLD 'EM

Control your own destiny or someone else will.
- Jack Welch, former General Electric CEO

AS A MANAGER, SOMETIMES YOU will have to do the unpleasant. No matter how hard you try to motivate and coach, you will have people who just won't respond. There will be excuse makers and there will be lazy people who just don't try. If you don't take action, as Mr. Welch says, someone else will, and it could be action against you for not doing the job you were hired to do.

It's OK to give people the benefit of the doubt. Too many leaders come into a situation and just start swinging the ax, destroying lives and careers without regard to the consequences of their actions. Life has a funny way of paying these people back. The longer you live, the more you see it. You, as a manager, must carefully assess each person on your team and ensure that you don't hastily swing your own ax.

But as a leader and a manager, there will come the time, after you given people the chance to be better, that you get no response. It's time to move on them. You will need to let them go. It is your responsibility to them, to the company, and to yourself to take action when such people just refuse to do what it takes to improve themselves and their performance.

You must also be able to determine if performance is due to circumstances beyond a rep's control, or if a lack of ability or lack of effort is the cause of failing performance. Finally, you must also be careful not to hang in there too long with someone. There is a fine line between giving someone the benefit of the doubt and just not having the guts or nerve to let them go.

Sometimes change is not only good for the company but also for the salesperson. Sometimes people get complacent in their jobs and could be doing much better simply by making a change, finding something to be passionate about. Sometimes if you let someone go, he will go on to incredible new heights in his life and career.

You wish he/she had peaked while working for you, but unfortunately, they fell into the trap of being safe and secure. By giving them a kick in the pants, you might awaken the greatness within. Sometimes it takes the hard, cold reality of unemployment to really get someone's attention.

> *Motivation is simple. You eliminate those who are not motivated.*
>
> *- Lou Holtz, college football coach*

45

THE POWER OF POSITIVE THINKING

Change your thoughts and you change your world.
- Dr. Norman Vincent Peale

*Formulate and stamp indelibly on your mind a mental picture
of yourself as succeeding. Hold this picture tenaciously. Never
permit it to fade. Your mind will seek to develop the picture. Do
not build up obstacles in your imagination.*
- Dr. Norman Vincent Peale

THE POWER OF POSITIVE THINKING is the key to success in any job, career, or
aspect of life. It is one of the most powerful ways to become a top manager.

Whatever you focus your mind on will eventually become a reality in your
life. If you believe your salespeople are worthless and lazy, they won't work hard
and will underperform. If you believe that your division or region has more
difficult problems than others around the country, then you and your team will
fall into a mire of making excuses and failing. Believe that you are a great
manager who can lead your team to success, and there is a high probability you
will. Keep your attitude positive for a few years, and you will likely have an
overflow of success and blessings in your life.

*A positive mental attitude (PMA) is the single most important
principle of the science of success!*
- Napoleon Hill

Look for the glass to be half full. The power of a positive mental attitude
will blow you away. You will attract all the right customers, all the right
salespeople, all the right opportunities, and all the right people to help you and

your team achieve your goals. Stop looking at things in your life negatively and only positive will come about.

> *Change the way you look at things and the things you look at change.*
>   *- Dr. Wayne Dyer, philosopher*

> *There is very little difference in people. But that little difference makes a big difference. The little difference is attitude. The big difference is whether it is positive or negative.*
>   *- W. Clement Stone, author and salesman*

No matter what you do in life, if you want to be successful you'll have to maintain a positive attitude. The minute negativity creeps into your mind, flush it out because it will be your demise if you let it grow. If you look at most of the setbacks you've had in your life and career, you will usually find that something caused your attitude to go south.

In addition, you must foster, encourage, and demand a positive attitude in your team. It is human nature to look at all that is going wrong or that is wrong rather than focus on all that is right and good. If you allow one team member to turn the attitudes of the other members to the negative, it will be a terrible disease that will destroy your momentum and success. For this reason, it is imperative to help this rep change his/her attitude. Let's talk more about this in the next chapter.

------◆------

Dean:

Reflecting on my life, I can absolutely tell you that the biggest challenges and setbacks have occurred when I allowed myself to become negative. After 9/11, I had some setbacks. It was a very negative time in my career when the rep I mentioned earlier tried to take my job. I didn't enjoy working for my mentor at the time, and it got me down. It is often said that what you think about most will come into your life. If you think negative thoughts, negative things will occur. It is amazing that the way I have turned things around was to get back to thinking positively and to get out of or solve any negative situations.

I'm not a quitter, and I hung in there with that job for about a year and a half too long (it was also a year after this personal attack occurred). Finally one day, my wife asked me, "Why do you stay there? You aren't happy, and you haven't been yourself." She lifted a load off my shoulders, and soon I was offered another job at a fantastic J&J division where I achieved even more success than before. But, I can honestly say that I would not trade that year and a half of challenges for anything. It made me a better manager and human being.

46

HOW TO DEAL WITH AVERAGE REPS

My experience with people is that they generally do what you expect them to do.
                    - Mary Kay Ash, founder, Mary Kay Cosmetics

IF YOU WANT YOUR TEAM to perform at an above-average level, if you want to win awards as region or division of the year, if you want your salespeople to be the best they can be, win awards, and make a lot of commission, then you've got to raise the bar for them. You cannot allow it to be acceptable for them to constantly hit 85%, 90%, and 95% of quota or forecast. If you do the forecast properly, everyone should be able to hit the forecast and ultimately hit and surpass their annual quota. You can't reward people for being below forecast or quota. Now, if the entire nation is at 80% of quota and your team members are performing at an average of 90-95% of quota, maybe the company quota was off, and the percentages are not so bad.

Some managers accept that a certain percentage of their team will be average. If you want to be a top manager, you cannot accept average performance. Why should you? If you aren't average, why should you accept that others are willing to perform at an average level? You don't have to become a raging bull, but there are very professional ways to let people know what you expect and being average is not one of them.

The first thing you should do, at least on a weekly basis, is announce where people stand against the monthly quota and forecast. List them in the order of rank. Don't just point out how they are performing overall, but also let them know how they are doing in the focus products as well. If you don't want to call out everyone's numbers, just call out those who are trending over forecast. At the end of the month, recap how everyone did for the month and how they are doing against quota for the year. At the end of each month, also rank people as to how they are doing from a growth standpoint, year over year. Mention the total volume people have sold for the year. Give a ranking as to how people are doing from a percent growth for the month over the prior year month. Also, state their YTD percent growth year over year. Send a recap of your voicemail in an e-mail. Point out the outstanding job people are doing. Never embarrass a sales rep in public by reprimanding the rep in front of his/her peers. Don't embarrass reps with the sales rankings by commenting on poor performance. By ranking each person in the various categories, it becomes very obvious as to who is working and who is not.

People do not like to hear that they are at the bottom of any ranking. This is one way to motivate people to do better. Also, you might have a sales rep of the month award. Recognize the most outstanding rep with a gift certificate or some reward for being the best of the month. There's no reason why you can't also have a division or region sales rep of the year award.

Have fun and help the reps to have fun at their job. Making their lives miserable will only motivate them for a short time. After a while they will become immune to your style of intimidation and will just leave the company. Some companies have a philosophy of managing by intimidation. They burn and churn their salespeople for two or three years and then expect them to leave. These are usually entry-level jobs, and that philosophy may work in particular situations. In fact, people coming out of such tough environments and still succeed develop very thick skins and tend to do very well in a more professional environment. The challenge for these companies is constant turnover. Sometimes they recognize they will have high turnover, managing with the knowledge that they will get high production for about two years before the sales rep will leave. We've never created intimidation environments, nor would we want to do so.

In dealing with average salespeople, get them to perform at a higher level and don't let up on them. Very few average people will change their ways and go from being average performers to being top performers, so if you want to be a top manager you've got to accept the fact that you may have to replace them eventually. It is not your fault that they accept being average or below average. If you raise the bar by increasing quota, then eventually average performance will become below average. They will either leave or you will have the grounds to put them on a performance plan and eventually let them go.

Remember, the company is looking to you to get the best out of your people and grow the business. It is not your fault if someone chooses a life of mediocrity. Hopefully, you can motivate, coach, and inspire people to perform at the highest possible level, but know that you will not be able to "save" everyone. Not everyone will be up for the challenge.

47

PUT YOUR REPS FIRST; GIVE THEM THE GLORY

Don't worry when you are not recognized, but strive to be worthy of recognition.
- Abraham Lincoln, 16th U.S. president

THIS IS HARD FOR SOME managers. Some managers are insecure about their jobs, themselves and how they are doing as managers. In order to cover themselves, they take all the glory from their salespeople. If they do joint calls on customers and convert business, they are the first to run back to the region director or VP of sales and report how they helped so-and-so rep convert x amount of business.

Instead of taking the approach of running to the VP to tell them how great YOU are, give your salespeople all the glory. If you take care of your salespeople, help them succeed, and give them the glory, all the recognition and success you ever wanted will come your way. Even if you have closed a deal for a rep, send out a message letting your team and even your mentor know what a great job the sales rep did on the call. Don't mention that you were the catalyst. First, the sales rep will know what you did, and his/her respect and loyalty will grow. The rep will be astonished that you gave him/her all the credit. It will help raise the rep's desire to do even better. His/her performance will get even better. Talk about developing loyalty! It doesn't get any better.

In the end, when your team wins region of the year or you become manager of the year, you will receive all the recognition you deserve and desire. One by one, your team members will tell others what a great manager you are and how much you've helped them and how much they love working for you. It's funny how life often works. When you are arrogant and selfish, you will rarely get rewards and awards, but when you are helpful and low key, it all flows your way.

A word of caution with average or below average sales reps: you must be sure to document the good and the bad in their performance.

Always remember that your success and your income are generated by your people. Recognize them, take care of them, and you'll be taken care of. You will earn the highest commission, you will win the awards, and you will get the promotions, if you want them. **Give the glory and you will receive the glory**.

———◆———

Dean:

I found that the more credit, thanks, and glory you give to others, the more recognition you will receive in the end. If you recognize your salespeople and let them bask in the glory, they will perform better for you. In the end, you will win awards for region manager of the year, and there will be no denying your excellence as a manager. When you consistently reward your team with praise and shine the spotlight on them rather than on yourself, it will be one ingredient that will help you to become a consistent, high performing manager. No one likes to work for a self-centered, attention-grabbing manager. You can spot those people a mile away, and not only do their salespeople disrespect them but also their peers. It's funny how some people rush so fast to take credit, yet in the end it does them no good. Give the credit and glory to your salespeople but also to all the support people who help your team on a daily basis: customer service, national account managers, the warehouse people, and anyone else who helps you do your job.

———◆———

Dave:

I have had the opportunity to lead five different teams to a division of the year award. My first team is the one from which I learned the most about managing. I took too much of the credit. I was young, immature, and wanted to look good to upper management. After getting home and hanging the award on my wall, guilt started to set in. It wasn't about me; it was about the team. Yes, I was part of the team, but THEY did the work, made the sales, kept the customers happy, asked for and received large orders at year end. After I learned that the glory should have been given to each member of my team for their individual contributions to the team's success, I grew up and began to mature as a manager.

As a side note, all the awards I have ever won or shared with my team are in boxes in my attic at home. I learned not to be showy. My peers knew that I had won many times. I didn't need to rub it in or show up someone else.

—————◆—————

Morris Becker's CODE OF LIFE

When the age of retirement dawned upon me, a mixed feeling of anticipation came along with it. My anticipation slowly and surely marched by, as I tasted of it and found it sweet. The flavor of my early dreams, however, was no more. I am 67 years old with fixed and settled ideas, also with a code to steer me right.

I found that CODE OF LIFE only in parts all through my younger life, in the home, in the school, in the factory, in the office, and in books. I imbibed it and made it mine, and it was finally shaped and formed through constant practice.

I learned many things from all sources and practiced them faithfully. As a result, I now enjoy peace of mind. As I reflect on the code, I am now giving it.

What is my code and how did I obtain it? Some who read it may find it of some value, especially those who are of a constitution like my own.

First, what is my code? To begin with it, I always noticed that a person's actions are always held up in the balance and the scales judged if the man or woman plays the game fairly. Some are found who always cheat a little bit; they think that they are smart, and no one can read or understand the balance of the scales. As a result, they attract their like and the competition to cheat one another becomes a mutual attraction; needless to say, the persons who like to see the scales balanced find those persons undesirable company and treat them according to their worth.

There are others who wouldn't cheat in the slightest but would not give a fraction over than what was really bargained for. They watch the balance of the scale, and they will not yield a fraction over to anybody.

And there are still others who will smilingly give you more than the balance of the scale will indicate. I say, smilingly, because it causes them to smile back when they see the scales' balance, and it is in their favor. It brings not only a reaction of smiles but good will as well.

My code is to do a little more and better than I bargained for. Psychologically, I create an atmosphere that will cause one to smile and react accordingly.

The moral of the story: Do more for your sales reps; put them first, give them the glory, and it will come back to you tenfold.

48

KEEP AN OPEN MIND TO WHAT OTHERS ARE SAYING

Every man I meet is in some way my superior, and I can learn of him.

- Ralph Waldo Emerson

NO MATTER HOW GOOD A manager you are, you will never be right 100% of the time. A great leader has the ability to change directions, change his/her mind, and be open to listening to what his sales representatives, customers, other managers, and his and his mentors are saying. Don't be stubborn in life, period. Be open to new ideas and continually work to grow.

Understand that your business will change. What worked three years ago may not be working now. Your product may be maturing, or competitors may be in vast number. You and your team will need to adjust and adapt your sales approach on an annual basis. Be open to the fact that the market conditions are changing. That doesn't mean you should use that as an excuse as to why you are losing business.

You should use it as a reason to stay on top of your game, on top of your customers, and on top of the market. The leaders and companies that adapt the fastest have the best chance at continual success well into the future.

◆

Dean:

Regardless how smart you think you are, how smart I think I am, or how smart upper management thinks they are, the reality is that the sales reps are on the front line, every day, with customers, and they will have their fingers on the pulse of what is happening in the market usually before anyone else does. Yes, average and below-average salespeople may be making excuses saying prices are too high or customers don't like certain products, but you need to be listening to your top people. If they concur with what some of the average people are saying, there is probably some validity to it. It's better to stay in front of the curve as a company instead of always trying to play catch-up. Listen to what people are saying.

Shortly after arriving at one company, many of my reps and other reps around the company were claiming a certain trend in the marketplace. Rather than listen, the company chose to ignore it. Before you knew it, the market had done a total 360, and this company was left struggling in the dust. They could have reacted but failed to listen to the field.

———◆———

Dave:

Ask your team from time to time, "How am I doing?" Insist they be honest with you. If you want to continue to improve . . . you need feedback.

> *People will flood you with ideas if you let them.*
> *- Peter Smith, General Signal*

49

OLD-TIMERS

Sales Rep #1:   Is your job secure?

Sales Rep #2:   Oh, sure. It's me they can do without.

SOME COMPANIES WANT TO HIRE "young bucks" and have no interest in older, more tenured salespeople. The belief is that as people get older, have children, and get a few dollars in the bank, they will tend to not work quite as hard, their priorities change, and they'll lose that "fire in the belly." This usually happens to the average people, but they were average from the beginning. They just move to being less than average. But the great representatives usually continue being great and in fact, get better with age. They learn how to develop friendships and relationships much faster. They know all the shortcuts to get in to see customers, and they pick up new products extremely fast. Don't overlook strong tenured salespeople. The bottom line is that 60-70% of all sales reps are average whether they are younger or older. Just find the top 10% to hire and you'll do great. Have we said that already?

Interesting facts from Motley Fool to consider when passing up that 50⁺-year-old sales rep:

- ◆ The average 50-year-old has $42,797 saved.
- ◆ The average net worth (assets minus debts) of a 55-64-year-old is $45,447.
- ◆ 45% of Americans have saved nothing for retirement, including 40% of Baby Boomers.
- ◆ 38% don't actively save for retirement at all.

So the fact is, that 50-year-old may have more incentive to work hard and sell a lot of product over a 30-year-old who has his whole career ahead of him/her.

On the other hand, when you do have an average tenured sales representative, and he/she starts to become less than average, you need to ensure you document the rep's performance meticulously. You don't want an age discrimination charge against you or the company. The rep owes it to you to give you his/her best, and you owe it to your company to ensure each rep gives it. If not, you must do what you must to move the rep along. It's not fun and no one likes it, but removing below-average salespeople, no matter how old they are or how long they've been around, is part of your job.

Dean:

It comes back to being very careful about getting tunnel vision and missing opportunities to hire great salespeople. They come in all shapes, sizes, and ages. There is nothing wrong with trying to stick to a basic formula, but be open-minded enough to know when you have a superstar staring you in the face and he/she doesn't fit your mold. I've had super reps who have worked for me who were over 50, and I have had great reps who worked for me who were just a few years out of college. Remember Karma. She follows you everywhere. Discriminate against older salespeople and managers, and some day you may find yourself on the other end of that sort of discrimination. You may get turned out to pasture before you want to be.

Dave:

One of my last hires in the medical device business was a gentleman whom I had known almost 25 years. This guy has been a superstar everywhere he has been. He didn't work as hard as your normal 30- to 35-year-old who has a lot to prove.

However, he is the most proficient person I have ever had at building relationships, converting business, and maintaining business. He is a real sales professional. He could accomplish more in a five- to six-hour day than most could in a 10-hour day. Still, he loved his job so much, he worked 10-

12 hours, a day, and I felt like I had hired TWO people to cover one territory!

The interesting part of this is that I did not pursue him. He had been asking me for several years for the opportunity to join our organization. I struggled with letting him in because in my mind, he was too old. He convinced me to at least meet with him. That did it. After about 10-15 minutes, I knew we had to hire this guy! His statement to me that made an instant impression was: "If you will give me a chance, I will prove to you that I still have it and be like a lottery pick in the NBA draft for you." Boy was he ever right, and was I jacked up about hiring him once I saw him in action! He blew me away with his drive, determination, attitude, and mentoring ability for the younger superstars I had on my team. What a great example he was setting every day! He raised the bar in my division. I was fortunate that this individual wanted to come to work for me and our organization.

Bottom line: What's it going to hurt to give an older sales professional an interview?

50

GET OUT AND WORK WITH EVERYONE

THIS IS NOT A RULE set in stone. The state of your division or region, the number of salespeople you must manage, and what is happening at your company will also dictate when and with whom you work. We are trying to say that you must get out and work with everyone, not just good reps or not just bad reps. Don't just work with your new reps and not just your tenured reps.

If, when you walk into your division, you have a bunch of new people just out of training, for a while you'll need to spend a tremendous amount of time with these new reps. Your tenured reps can keep things going for a month or two before you work with them. You need to get out and show your new people the ropes, making sure they can get a strong foundation and head start. Don't leave a new rep's preparation solely up to sales training and the field sales trainer.

Even if you are new and don't know the products well:

1) You need to go to sales training, too.

2) You still need to get out in the field with them and learn.

3) Show them you aren't afraid to roll up your sleeves.

4) You still need to do all the things a manager is supposed to do.

Even if you aren't an expert on the products, you can evaluate performance and how well the new rep is learning the products. If you are a medical sales manager, you need to get into cases and procedures with your reps. You need to cover cases sometimes without your reps. First, this will show your people you are really going to support them. Second, this will help you become an expert, too. Third, this will allow you to get to know your important customers. If some representatives leave, you'll have no problem maintaining relationships and getting into the accounts.

51

BE TRUTHFUL WITH YOUR PEOPLE

To be persuasive we must be believable; to be believable we must be credible; to be credible we must be truthful.
- Edward R. Murrow, journalist

TO LEAD A TEAM, YOUR salespeople must believe in you. Don't lie to them. Don't hide the truth. It's better to be honest, deliver bad news, and then work through the issues rather than try to hide the truth or situation through lies. If your salespeople catch you lying to them, you will lose their trust and their willingness to go into battle with or for you.

In addition, you must be truthful to with reps about their performance. You can't beat around the bush if they aren't performing acceptably. Be forthright and honest. The sooner you tell them the truth, the sooner they have a chance to turn things around and make it. Lie to them, tell them they are doing great, and you will set yourself up for problems should termination become necessary.

I have found that being honest is the best technique I can use. Right up front, tell people what you are trying to accomplish and what you're willing to sacrifice to accomplish it.
- Lee Iacocca

52

GIVE CLEAR DIRECTIONS

Ingenuity, plus courage, plus work equals miracles.
- Bob Richards, Olympic gold medalist

SALESPEOPLE ARE NOT IN THE military. They don't have to take direction just because you give it. People are more willing to do things if you explain the why. Don't be vague. Give clear, concise direction as to what you want, when you want it, and how you would like it. If your director asks that all your reps begin inputting customer information into a database, that will require a lot of time and will require reps to ask customers a lot of questions. Wouldn't you like to know why? Don't you think the reps would like to understand as well? What if your director asks you to get the information in all the big accounts yourself? Now you'll really want to know why, how, and when.

If it is YOU who is asking for something directly, make sure the questions have value. The information may help you do a better job of managing. Maybe the performance of the team is sliding, and you need to have a better understanding of what is going on in the division. Whatever it is you are asking for, whether the request comes from upper management or directly from you, your people deserve to understand why, when, and how.

Sometimes upper management asks for something that YOU don't agree with. Hopefully you work in an environment in which you can communicate your difference of opinion. Before you presume to speak for a group, though, be sure the other managers agree with your assessment (and will concur). Don't be an instigator, but be a leader and present why an idea isn't the best, or why another way to do something might be more effective.

If field management expresses concern about a certain report or task that upper management is requesting, then you may have to explain to your people why the information is needed. If any of your reps resists providing the report, explain to them that you need their help obtaining the information. Remind the reps that you go to bat for them, and, in this case, you need their help. If they still fail to do what you ask, then you have a bigger issue and may need to take corrective action.

The bottom line is people are more apt to do things, do them correctly, do them with thought, and do them on time if they understand why and how you want them done. Don't just give vague direction and expect to get good results. Give clear, concise direction. Make sure your direction is well understood and answer any questions. If you give unclear direction, you will get eight or nine different forms of the information you requested and 1) You'll have to ask for it again (people like to do things once). 2) You'll spend hours correcting the information yourself. Either way is inefficient.

In summary, when you ask your team members to do something, be sure to tell them: 1) what you want or need, 2) why you need it, 3) when you want it, and 4) suggestions as to how to do it. Sometimes you will need things to be very precise and uniform, and sometimes you can use information put together individually.

Remember to inspect what you expect. If you ask for a report or information by a certain date, make sure you receive it by that date. Also, make sure your reps know you inspect the information and then use it. Give feedback or a question indicating you read the reports. During your next field visit, review the information and discuss it. If it was information that upper management wanted, keep salespeople apprised of how the company is using that information to make the company stronger and better.

If you ask for information and never collect it, read it, use it, or give feedback, your team will begin to question if you care about their time and will eventually stop responding to your requests. Then you will have to deal with a whole new set of problems. If you actually use the information provided, people will do a much better job of completing your requests. But be careful. Don't be a manager who has his reps complete so many reports charts and graphs that they don't have time to sell. Remember, the more time a salesperson can be in front of the customer selling, the more products he/she will sell. Sometimes managers and companies forget this simple rule.

———◆———

Dean:

Entry-level sales jobs often require weekly call reports, which is totally understandable. It teaches discipline, goal-setting techniques, and basic selling skills. It also helps management stay on top of new salespeople. But for higher level sales, too much paperwork is often resented. One of my former employers even required tenured salespeople to fill out weekly call reports. Not only did most of the managers rarely read the reports, but also upper management didn't either. Several managers voiced the opinion that a monthly report format be initiated, and after about six months, the company agreed.

CONCLUSION

IF YOU HAVEN'T FIGURED IT out yet, management is a tremendously challenging, sometimes frustrating, yet incredibly rewarding occupation. Learn the art and science of being a strong leader and manager, and you will truly enjoy your life and career. Choose to use tactics that are counterproductive, and you will be miserable in your job.

When you accept the job of manager, you accept the job of problem solver. There will be tough decisions to make. There will be serious problems to solve. Sometimes people will be upset by the decisions you have to make to benefit the team as a whole. Before you accept a managerial position, you had better be sure you like the role of problem solver and that you can make tough decisions. Many people don't consider the responsibilities before taking the position. Managing is much more than getting everyone selling and working the same.

A good manager is leader, coach, teacher, cheerleader, and, yes, problem solver. Encourage your salespeople to come to you with solutions to problems, but many times you'll have to solve issues the reps can't. You'll have to be a problem solver on a large scale, balancing the needs of your salespeople, the customers, and the company. You must stand up for what is right and take all three into consideration. Be fair.

We have spent a combined 40+ years in management. If we didn't like it, we wouldn't have done it so long. But we are always learning, always looking for ways to be better and more effective. Remember that your salespeople are the ones who put food on your table. Just as managers aren't the enemy, sales reps or subordinates aren't the enemy. Treat them with respect. Work to develop and coach them. Motivate them, teach them, and help them in every way you can. When they don't perform, you'll have to school them, and in some cases, help them find the door. Hire great people. Hire the best people, and your life will be simple and fun. Hire the wrong people, and your life will be tough and not so fun.

Management isn't for everyone, but you don't have to be born a natural leader and manager. You can learn to be great if you work at it. We hope this book has provided some insight and ideas for ways you can improve. We wish you all the success in the world.

Sincerely,

Dean Gould and Dave Goldin

Double, no triple our troubles and we'd still be better off than any other people on earth.

- Ronald Reagan, 40th U.S. president

www.ingramcontent.com/pod-product-compliance
Lightning Source LLC
Chambersburg PA
CBHW051959090426
42741CB00008B/1457

* 9 7 8 0 9 7 6 3 5 5 3 1 1 *